Caribbean Cooking

Caribbean Cooking

DEVINIA SOOKIA

CHARTWELL
BOOKS, INC.

A QUINTET BOOK

Published by Chartwell Books
A Division of Book Sales, Inc.
110 Enterprise Avenue
Secaucus, New Jersey 07094

This edition produced for sale
in the U.S.A., its territories
and dependencies only.

ISBN 0–7858–0024–7

This book was designed and produced by
Quintet Publishing Limited
6 Blundell Street
London N7 9BH

Creative Director: Richard Dewing
Designer: Fiona Akehurst
Project Editor: Katie Preston
Editor: Michelle Clark
Editorial Assistant: Anna Briffa
Illustrator: Amanda Green
Photographer: Andrew Sydenham
Home Economy: Cara Hobday and Nicola Fowler

Manufactured by Bright Arts (Pte) Ltd, Singapore.
Printed by Star Standard Industries (Pte) Ltd, Singapore.

DEDICATION
This book is dedicated to the two people who played
an important part in my life – my loving father Gayadeen and
my devoted husband Bashir.

Contents

The Bahamas

ATLA

Cuba

Caicos & Turks Islands

Cayman Islands

GREATER ANTILLES

Haiti

Dominican
Republic

Puerto
Rico

Jamaica

CARIBBEAN SEA

Aruba

Curaçao

Introduction

When Christopher Columbus reached the Caribbean islands in 1492, he thought he had found the Garden of Eden. He was overwhelmed by the beauty of the Islands: the richness of the vegetation, the variety of fruits, the exotic scented flowers, and the singing of the birds.

The chain of Caribbean islands, stretching 2,500 miles from the southern edge of Florida to the northern coast of Venezuela, consists of more than 7,000 islands. Some are little more than rocks in the sea, while others are very big – Cuba being the largest. The next largest island is Hispaniola, which comprises Haiti and the Dominican Republic, followed by Jamaica and Puerto Rico. These four islands and some 25 other large ones, such as Trinidad, Guadeloupe, Martinique, Barbados, St. Lucia and Antigua, are known as the Caribbean islands, the West Indies, or the Antilles (a name given by fourteenth-century Europeans to a group of imaginary islands in the Atlantic).

One of the most exciting aspects of Caribbean culture is its

Islands

St Martin

Saba

St Eustatius

Antigua

St Kitts

Montserrat

Nevis

Guadeloupe

LESSER ANTILLES

Dominica

Martinique

St Lucia

Barbados

St Vincent

Grenada

Tobago

Trinidad

cuisine. In the Caribbean, "creole" is defined as "mixed and born on the islands." Caribbean cooking can thus be termed "creole cuisine." Caribbean dishes are spicy mixtures of meats, fish, and vegetables. The exotic fruits of the islands are coconuts, guavas, mangoes, papayas, pineapples, bananas, custard apples, star apples, soursops, mamey apples, shaddock, tamarind, ugli and passion fruits, jackfruits, and avocados. Vegetables found on the islands are christophenes, eggplants, pumpkin, okras, plantains, breadfruits, and ackee. The peoples of the Caribbean eat a lot of root vegetables such as yams, cassava, sweet potatoes, and dasheen. The fruits of the tropical sea are the local spiny lobster, conch, shrimp, crabs, kingfish, and other exotic seafood.

Caribbean culture and cuisine have been shaped by four waves of settlers that affected all the islands. The Caribbean islands have been influenced by the Amerindians (Arawaks and Caribs), Europeans (Spanish, British, French, and Dutch), Africans, and Orientals (Indians and Chinese).

Around 2,000 years ago, the native inhabitants of the region, the Arawak and the Carib tribes, who originated from Venezuela and Guyana, settled in the Caribbean islands. They were dispersed by European settlers in the form of Spanish soldiers, English pirates, Dutch merchants, Irishmen, Scotsmen, and Frenchmen who left Europe following the voyages of Christopher Columbus. The Europeans later brought African slaves across from the Congo, Guinea, and the Gold Coast to work in their Caribbean sugarcane plantations. The Africans were followed by Orientals, who came as indentured servants from China and India.

The first influence on the Caribbean islands was, therefore, a primitive one. The Amerindians were farmers who grew crops like maize, cassava (which they used to make bread), sweet potatoes, arrowroot, beans, and peppers. Others gathered wild fruits such as guavas, pineapples and cashew fruits, and fished or hunted. A favorite dish was pepperpot – a mixed meat and vegetable stew. Now pepperpot is made only with mixed meats, hot pepper, and cassareep (the boiled juice of grated cassava).

The Amerindians' food was not sufficient for the Europeans, so Columbus asked for flour, meat, oil, vinegar, and wine to be sent over from Spain. The Spanish colonists brought

Right *Preparations for a feast, Grenada.*

with them many fruits, vegetables, and crops that, funnily enough, we now associate with the Caribbean, such as breadfruit, limes, oranges, mangoes, bananas, coconut, tamarind, sugarcane, ginger, coffee, and rice. Several Spanish dishes still feature in Caribbean cuisine, such as escovitch (pickled fish) and baccalaitos or stamp and go (salt cod fish cakes). Barbados has retained much of the British influence. Jug jug – traditionally served at Christmas – was brought to the island by Scottish people exiled after plotting rebellion in 1685. It is a version of the Scots dish known as haggis, and is made from salted meats, pigeon peas, herbs, and ground millet. The islands of Guadeloupe and Martinique are still part of France, and have a strong French flavor to their cooking. The Dutch have given the Caribbean one of its most interesting dishes – keshy yana (shrimp-filled Edam cheese).

The third wave – the African slaves – also greatly influenced Caribbean cuisine. The slaves brought with them pigeon peas, yams, okra, and taro. More importantly, they developed a style of cooking that is the basis of Caribbean cooking today.

10

Right *Sunset at Negril, Jamaica.*

As they were given only very small portions of salted meat and fish, they started to supplement their diet by growing their own food. As the food given to them had no taste, they found ingenious ways in which to flavor it with seasonings and pungent spices. Today, the main ingredient in the English-speaking islands for a stew is "a bunch of sive," which is made up of scallions tied in a bunch with parsley, coriander leaves, and thyme. The Spanish-speaking islands use "sofrito" – a sauce made from annatto seeds, coriander leaves, green peppers, onions, garlic, and tomatoes. Ginger, nutmeg, cloves, allspice, cinnamon and hot pepper are widely used on all the islands. Many of the traditional dishes have survived, such as callaloo – crab and greens soup.

The fourth influence on Caribbean food came in the early 1800s. There was pressure from England on the European colonists to free their slaves and, in 1848 and 1838 respectively, the French and English colonies granted emancipation to their slaves. Although they were then offered wages for their work, many ex-slaves refused to work in the fields, especially in Trinidad. Plantation owners, desperately needing a labor force, transported large numbers of indentured servants from India and China. As a result, curry gradually became as much a Caribbean dish as it is an Indian one. Roti or dhalpouri is another favorite in Trinidad and Jamaica. Chinese spare ribs, vegetables, and noodles are popular dishes in Trinidad. Maybe this also explains why, despite the variety of vegetables grown in the Caribbean, such as breadfruit, tannia, eddoes, cassava, sweet potatoes and plantains, which are eaten ripe *and* green, rice is also a very important food for many West Indians. It is served at almost every meal with meat, fish, and vegetables.

When we talk of Caribbean cooking, the food of Guyana and Surinam must be included. Although geographically these two countries are in South America, culturally they form part of the Caribbean.

Above *The Willemstad Easter festival, Curaçao.*

Left *Tropical Beach.*

13

Cooks Notes

*N*owadays we see more and more exotic fruits and vegetables in the shops. Plantains, cassava, coconuts, mangoes, avocados, carambolas, guavas, papaya, and pineapples can be obtained in any specialty West Indian shop, and many are now found in supermarkets, too. Even so, it is not always obvious how to recognize, choose, and prepare many of these fruits and vegetables, so here are some tips.

ACKEE

Ackee is the fruit of an evergreen tree introduced into Jamaica from West Africa. It is reddish-yellow in color, and when ripe it bursts open to display shiny black seeds covered by a creamy-yellow flesh – this is the only edible section, and it has a soft texture resembling scrambled eggs. The fruit must *only* be eaten ripe – unripe *and* overripe ackee can be poisonous.

ALLSPICE

This flavoring is also known as pimento seed. It is the dark reddish-brown berry of a tree indigenous to Jamaica. After the berries are dried in the sun, they look like large peppercorns, but the scent and flavor are similar to a blend of cinnamon, cloves, and nutmeg.

ANNATTO

A rusty red dried seed from the tropical annatto tree. It is used to color and flavor cooking oil.

ARROWROOT

A white starchy powder obtained from the underground stalk of a plant grown mainly in the Caribbean island of St. Vincent. It is used for thickening soups, sauces, and stews.

AVOCADO

It is commonly known as pear throughout the Caribbean as it is a pear-shaped fruit with creamy flesh and a thick green skin. Avocados can be bought when still firm. If you want to test the ripeness of an avocado, put it in the palm of your hand and squeeze it gently; when it yields to gentle pressure, it is ready to eat.

To prepare an avocado, cut it in half lengthways. Gently twist the halves apart to loosen the stone. Remove the stone with a knife. Rub the exposed flesh with lemon or lime juice to prevent it discoloring.

BAKES

Fried biscuits – a specialty of Trinidad.

BEANS

Islanders use the term peas for both peas and beans. Rice 'n' Peas is a dish made with rice and kidney beans or pigeon peas.

BREADFRUIT

A large round or oval green fruit used as a vegetable. It is best used when the skin is green rather than brown. The central core should be removed and the cream-colored flesh eaten as a starchy vegetable, boiled, roasted, or fried.

CALLALOO

The name given to the leaves of the dasheen or taro plant with which Callaloo is made.

CASHEW

An evergreen tree and shrub native to the West Indies. It bears a reddish, pear-shaped cashew apple, from the bottom of which grows the kidney-shaped nut; this is edible only when roasted.

CASSAREEP

This is an essential part of the stew known as pepperpot. It is the juice obtained from grated cassava and flavored with cinnamon, cloves, and brown sugar.

To make 6 tablespoons, you need 2 lb of young cassava root. Peel the brown bark off with a small sharp knife to reveal the white flesh of the cassava root. Cut the cassava root in half, and finely grate half of it into a deep bowl lined with a double thickness of dampened muslin or cheesecloth. Bring the ends of the cloth together to enclose the pulp, and twist very tightly to squeeze the cassava juice into the bowl. Discard the pulp. Grate and squeeze the rest of the cassava in the same way. Pour the liquid into a small frying pan and cook it over a medium heat for about 1 minute, stirring constantly, until the cassareep is smooth and thick. Cassareep is made fresh each time you need it.

CASSAVA

Also known as yuca, manioc, tapioca, and mandioca. It is a long, irregularly shaped root with a dark brown, rough, bark-like skin and hard white starchy flesh. It is an important item in the diet of many West Indians, and can be eaten boiled, baked, or fried.

CHRISTOPHENE

Also known as cho-cho, choyote, chayote, and tropical squash. This is a pear-shaped fruit with a single large stone in the center. The skin varies in color from white to pale yellow or bright green. The flesh is cooked as a vegetable, and has a taste similar to zucchini or vegetable marrow.

COCONUT

When you buy a coconut, shake it to make sure it has liquid inside – this is a sign that the coconut is fresh.

To open the coconut, puncture two of its "eyes" – the darker dots on one end – with a small, sharp knife or an ice pick. Drain all the liquid from the coconut, then tap the whole surface of the shell lightly with a hammer. Now give the shell a sharp blow with the hammer. This will open the coconut, and the meat will now come away from the shell.

How to make coconut milk

Grate the coconut meat. Measure the coconut and stir in an equal amount of hot, but not boiling, water. Cover a bowl with a piece of muslin or cheesecloth, and strain the coconut through the cloth, pressing down hard on the coconut with a wooden spoon to extract as much liquid as possible. If you measure 1¼

cups of coconut meat to 1¼ cups of water, you should produce 1¼ cups of coconut milk.

CONCH

Known as lambi in the Caribbean. It is an edible sea snail with big horns.

CORIANDER

Known as Chinese parsley or cilantro. It is an aromatic herb, and has a pungent flavor.

CUMIN

It is the yellowish-brown seed of a plant from the parsley family. It is aromatic, and is available whole or ground.

DASHEEN

Also known as taro and cocoyam. It is a tropical plant cultivated for both its underground tubers, which are eaten boiled, roasted or baked, and for its large leaves – known as callaloo leaves – which are used in Callaloo. If dasheen leaves are not available, fresh spinach is a good substitute.

EDDOES

A root vegetable related to dasheen. The underground tubers are similar, though the leaves cannot be eaten.

15

EGGPLANT
Some eggplants are large, oval-shaped, and purple; others are small and round, or small and long with striped purple skin. It is a vegetable which can be cooked on its own, or with meat and fish.

FLYING FISH
An unusual silver-blue winged fish with a white, slightly salty flesh and a large number of bones. It is found off the coasts of Barbados.

GHEE
Clarified butter – butter with the milk solids removed – that tolerates high temperatures without burning.

HOT PEPPERS
Hot peppers vary in hotness, but you must always be very careful when handling them: they can burn your skin and irritate your eyes, so wear rubber gloves when preparing them.

To prepare hot peppers, rinse them in cold water, then pull out the stalks, cut them in half, and remove the seeds. If the ribs inside the pods are thin, leave them as they are, but if they are firm, remove them with a sharp knife.

To take some of the heat out of hot peppers, soak them in cold, salted water for an hour before using them.

MANGO
The mango is a tropical fruit much used in Caribbean cooking but also delicious eaten raw. The ripe fruit varies in color from green to bright red. Mangoes are not easy to eat unless you known how to remove the stone. Place the mango flat side down on a board. Cut a thick slice from the top of the fruit as near to the stone as possible. Turn the fruit over. Repeat with the other side. The two halves can then be eaten by scooping out the flesh. The juicy flesh still attached to the stone can be cut off in chunks.

MAWBY BARK
The bark of a tropical tree which has a bitter taste. It is used to make a refreshing drink in the Caribbean.

METHI LEAVES
Also known as fenugreek leaves, methi leaves are taken from a leguminous plant with aromatic seeds.

OKRAS
Known as gumbo, ochro, bamie or lady's fingers, this plant produces pod-like fruits about 4 inches long. Each pod is oblong in shape and pointed at one end, with a soft and sticky interior. The pod is cooked as a vegetable.

PALM HEART
Tender, ivory-colored shoots obtained from the core at the crown or top of the palm tree. Palm hearts are used as a vegetable or a salad ingredient.

PAPAYA
Also known as pawpaw, this is a large melon-like fruit that ranges in length from 3 to 20 inches. The fruit has a green skin when raw, and a yellow skin, sweet yellow flesh, and black seeds when ripe.

The soft skin contains papain, which is a meat tenderizer. A deliciously simple starter is to serve papaya with ginger.

PASSION FRUIT
An egg-shaped fruit about 2 inches long. When ripe, the leathery skin becomes wrinkled and purple in color. To eat, it must be cut in half and the juicy yellow seeds scooped out with a spoon.

PIGEON PEAS
Known as goongoo or gunga peas. They are the size of a small garden pea. Young pigeon peas are green, and are available in cans.

PINEAPPLE

One of the most familiar tropical fruits. The best way to peel a pineapple is to remove the spiky leaves from the top, then make slanting cuts downwards to remove the skin. It can then be sliced or cut into wedges, removing the core, though, if the pineapple is very ripe, the core should not be removed as it has a very good flavor and texture.

PLANTAIN

A fruit of the banana family, similar in shape but larger and not so sweet; it must be cooked before being eaten. It can be green or yellow in color according to ripeness.

Plantains are difficult to handle as the thick skin clings to the fruit. To remove the peel, cut off the ends of the plantain and then halve the trimmed plantain with a sharp knife. Make four evenly spaced lengthways slits in the skin of each half, cutting through to the flesh from one end to the other. Then, starting at the corner of one slit, lift the skin away, one strip at a time.

SALT BEEF

Beef preserved in salt. It can be eaten in bread or in recipes.

SALT COD

Originally brought to the Caribbean as food for slaves by the Colonists. Of all the salted fish, cod seems to have the best flavor. To remove the salt, wash well and soak for several hours or overnight in cold water.

SEA EGG

The Island name for a white sea urchin.

SORREL

A tropical flower grown throughout the islands. Its fleshy sepal has a faintly acid taste and is used in making drinks, jams, and jellies.

SOURSOP

A large, dark green, heart-shaped fruit with a spiny skin. Its pithy flesh has black seeds and is slightly acidic. It is often used to make drinks or ice creams.

SWEET POTATO

A tuberous vegetable whose skin color ranges from yellow to reddish brown and pink. The flesh may be white, yellow or orange, and can be eaten boiled, baked, fried, or roasted. Ideal for both sweet and savory dishes.

TANNIA

A root vegetable of the same family as the dasheen. It is the size of a large baking potato, with dark brown bark-like skin. The firm flesh is white and has a nutty flavor.

TARO

Another name for dasheen.

YAM

These are tubers that grow under large vines known as tropical creepers. Although very like the sweet potato, the yam is not as sweet; the flesh is moister in texture, and the skin is red or brown.

17

SEASONING AND MARINATING

Seasoning and marinating are essential in Caribbean cooking. Nothing is cooked without being seasoned a few hours before and left to marinate. Cheap cuts are transformed if they are left to marinate in spices overnight.

~Except for steak, meats such as beef, pork, veal, lamb, venison, chicken, hare, or rabbit must be allowed to marinate for at least 4 hours before cooking.

~A good marinade for meat is made from 1¼ cups cold water, 2 crushed garlic cloves, generous pinches of salt and freshly ground black pepper, 1 tablespoon vinegar, and 1 teaspoon chopped thyme.

~Fish must be cleaned well in cold water. If it is to be cooked the same day, wash it well with lime or lemon juice under cold running water. If not, wash it with cold water and vinegar. Remove the scales and any remaining traces of blood, then cut it into steaks or fillets, or leave whole as required.

~For the best results, marinate fish for at least 4 hours or overnight. A good marinade for fish is 1 finely chopped scallion or green onion, 1 teaspoon chopped hot pepper, generous pinches of salt and freshly ground black pepper, 1 teaspoon chopped thyme, 1 tablespoon vinegar, 2 whole cloves, 3 crushed garlic cloves, and cold water.

Soups

CALLALOO ~ Barbados

PUMPKIN SOUP ~ Antigua

PEPPERPOT ~ Trinidad

BLACK BEAN SOUP ~ Cuba

CHICKEN AND VEGETABLE SOUP ~ Aruba

TOMATO AND SWEET POTATO SOUP ~ Dominica

PEANUT SOUP ~ St. Vincent

BREADFRUIT SOUP ~ Grenada

SOPITO ~ Curaçao

GREEN PIGEON PEA SOUP ~ Puerto Rico

Barbados

Callaloo

Crab and Greens Soup

SERVES 6

½ lb dasheen leaves or
1 lb fresh spinach
2½ tbsp butter or margarine
1 onion, finely chopped
2 garlic cloves, crushed
1 fresh hot pepper, deseeded and finely chopped
(see page 16)
¼ lb okra, trimmed and sliced
1 sprig fresh thyme
3¾ cups chicken stock
1¼ cups coconut milk (see page 15)
salt and freshly ground black pepper
½ lb crabmeat, fresh, canned or frozen
dash of hot pepper sauce

20

~ Wash the dasheen or spinach leaves, drain
and then shred them.

~ Heat the butter or margarine in a large
saucepan over a medium heat. Add the onion
and garlic and cook for 5 minutes, stirring
occasionally until soft and golden. Add the
hot pepper, okra and thyme, and cook for
5 more minutes, stirring constantly. Stir in
the dasheen or spinach leaves and cook for
3 minutes, turning them in the pan to ensure
they are evenly cooked. Pour the stock and
coconut milk over the leaves, season with salt
and freshly ground black pepper, and bring
to the boil. Then lower the heat, cover the
pan, and simmer for 30 minutes.

~ Add the crabmeat, and cook for 5 more
minutes until it has heated through. Taste
and adjust the seasoning if necessary, and stir
in the pepper sauce.

~ Serve on its own in warmed soup bowls or
with Cornmeal Dumplings.

Pumpkin Soup

SERVES 4–6

2 lb pumpkin, peeled, deseeded, and cut into 1-inch cubes
salt and freshly ground black pepper
2 tbsp butter or margarine
1 large onion, finely chopped
3 scallions, trimmed and finely chopped
3 tomatoes, skinned and chopped
1 cup coconut milk (see page 15)
¼ tsp freshly grated nutmeg
pinch of cayenne pepper
⅔ cup sour cream or yogurt

~Put the pumpkin in a saucepan and add enough water (about 3¾ cups) to cover, together with 1 teaspoon of salt. Bring to the boil, then lower the heat and simmer for 20 minutes.

~Drain and reserve the cooking liquid.

~Melt the butter or margarine in a clean saucepan over moderate heat. Add the onion and scallions, and fry them, stirring constantly, for 5 minutes, until they are soft and golden. Add the pumpkin, tomatoes, coconut milk, 3 cups of the pumpkin cooking liquid, half the nutmeg, a pinch of cayenne pepper, and salt and freshly ground black pepper. Bring to the boil, then lower the heat, cover, and simmer for 30 minutes.

~Remove the pan from the heat and leave it to cool slightly. Liquidize half the soup at a time in a blender, then return it to the pan. Heat it through for 5 minutes, then pour the soup into warmed soup bowls and swirl a little of the sour cream or yogurt on top. Sprinkle with the remaining nutmeg, and serve at once.

Pepperpot

Chicken and Meat Stew

SERVES 6 TO 8

3 lb boiling chicken, trimmed of fat and cut into 12 pieces
¹/₂ lb fresh pig's trotter
8 cups water
1¹/₂ tsp salt
3 lb boned pork or beef cut into 2-in cubes
6 tbsp cassareep (see page 15)
1 large onion, sliced
1¹/₂ tbsp brown sugar
2 whole, fresh hot peppers
4 whole cloves
2-in piece of cinnamon stick
¹/₄ tbsp dried thyme
2¹/₂ tsp malt vinegar

~Put the chicken, pig's trotter, and water into a large saucepan (the water should cover them by about an inch). Add the salt and bring to the boil over a low heat, skimming off any foam as it collects on the surface. Then, reduce the heat, partially cover the pan, and simmer for about 1 hour or until the chicken is cooked.

~Skim as much fat as possible from the surface of the soup. Stir in the pork or beef, cassareep, onion, brown sugar, hot peppers, cloves, cinnamon stick and thyme, and bring to the boil over a high heat. Lower the heat and simmer for 30 minutes, stirring occasionally, until the meat is cooked.

~Remove the cloves, cinnamon stick and hot peppers, stir in the vinegar and taste, adjusting the seasoning if necessary.

~Serve the soup with boiled yam, cassava, or potatoes as accompaniments.

Cuba

Black Bean Soup

SERVES 6

1 lb dried black beans
2½ tsp salt
3¾ cups chicken stock
1½ tbsp vegetable oil mixed with 1 tsp liquid annatto
(see page 14)
1 medium onion, finely chopped
1 fat garlic clove, finely chopped
½ lb lean cooked ham, finely chopped
1 large, firm, ripe tomato, peeled, deseeded and finely
chopped; or 8-oz can chopped tomatoes, drained
1½ tbsp malt vinegar
½ tsp ground cumin
freshly ground black pepper

24

~Wash the beans under cold running water and drain in a colander. Put the beans in a large saucepan together with the salt and enough water to cover the beans by 2 inches. Bring to the boil over a high heat, then reduce the heat, partially cover the pan, and simmer for 2 hours or until the beans are tender.

~Drain the beans, reserving the liquid, and leave them on one side to cool.

~Add enough chicken stock to the reserved cooking liquid from the beans to make 5 cups. Put half the cooked beans in a blender and grind, but not too finely. Grind the remaining beans. Mix the ground beans with the chicken and bean stock.

~Heat the oil in a large saucepan, add the onion and garlic, and cook for 5 minutes, stirring frequently. Stir in the ham, tomato, vinegar, cumin, bean and stock mixture, and freshly ground black pepper to taste. Bring to the boil, then lower the heat and simmer for 15 minutes. Taste to check the seasoning, adjusting if necessary.

~Serve the soup in bowls, together with slices of fresh bread.

Aruba

Chicken and Vegetable Soup

SERVES 6

3 lb chicken, cut into 8 pieces
6¼ pints chicken stock
4 large tomatoes, peeled, deseeded and chopped;
or 2 × 1-lb cans chopped tomatoes, drained
2 medium-sized corn cobs, cut into 3-in pieces
2 medium yams, peeled and chopped into 1-in thick slices
2 small potatoes, peeled and cut into 1-in thick slices
¼ lb pumpkin, peeled and diced
¾ cup fresh or frozen green peas
2 small hot peppers, deseeded and sliced thinly
(see page 16)
2½ tsp salt
freshly ground black pepper
1½ tbsp finely chopped fresh chives

~Put the chicken pieces and stock into a large saucepan, and bring to the boil over a high heat. Skim off the foam with a large spoon, then reduce the heat, partially cover, and simmer for 45 minutes.

~Skim the fat from the soup. Add the tomatoes, corn, yams, potatoes, pumpkin, peas, hot peppers, salt and freshly ground black pepper, and bring to the boil. Reduce the heat, and simmer for about 20 minutes or until the chicken and vegetables are cooked.

~Taste the soup, adjusting the seasoning if necessary. Stir in the chives, then serve immediately.

Tomato and Sweet Potato Soup

Peanut Soup

SERVES 6

1 tbsp oil
1 tbsp butter or margarine
2 onions, finely chopped
½ lb sweet potatoes, peeled and diced
1 lb tomatoes, skinned and finely chopped
2½ cups chicken stock
1 tsp salt
1 tsp chopped fresh thyme
juice and grated rind of 1 orange
juice and grated rind of 1 lemon or lime
freshly ground black pepper
slices of lemon, orange, and tomato to garnish

~Heat the oil and butter or margarine in a large saucepan. Add the onions, and cook them until they are soft.

~Add the sweet potatoes, tomatoes, chicken stock, salt, thyme, orange juice and rind, lemon or lime juice and rind, and freshly ground black pepper to taste. Bring to the boil, then lower the heat, cover the saucepan, and simmer for 25 minutes.

~Liquidize the soup in a blender, then return it to the saucepan and simmer for 5 more minutes to heat it through.

~Serve it in warmed soup bowls, garnished with a slice of tomato, orange, and lemon.

SERVES 4

¼ cup butter or margarine
1 onion, grated
1 celery stick, chopped
1 garlic clove, crushed
1 sprig fresh thyme, chopped
1 tbsp flour
3¾ cups chicken stock
½ cup crunchy peanut butter or 2¼ cups coarsely ground peanuts
2 cups milk
2 tsp salt
½ tsp freshly ground black pepper
¼ green pepper, deseeded and chopped

~Melt the butter or margarine in a large saucepan over a low heat. Add the onion, celery, garlic, and thyme. Cook for 5 minutes, stirring all the time, then gradually add the flour and stock, still stirring constantly. Increase the heat, then stir in the peanut butter or peanuts and cook for 10 minutes.

~Reduce the heat and add the milk, salt, and pepper. Simmer for 15 minutes.

~Serve very hot, garnished with the chopped green pepper.

26

Right *Peanut soup.*

Grenada

Breadfruit Soup

SERVES 6

4 tbsp butter or margarine
1 medium onion, finely chopped
1 fat garlic clove, crushed
6 oz fresh breadfruit, peeled, cored, and chopped
2¹/₂ cups chicken stock
1¹/₄ cups light cream
1 tsp salt
¹/₄ tsp freshly ground black pepper
2 tsp finely chopped fresh parsley

~ Melt the butter or margarine in a large saucepan. Add the onion and garlic and cook for 5 minutes, stirring until they are soft. Add the breadfruit and chicken stock and bring to the boil. Reduce the heat and simmer for 20 minutes, or until the breadfruit is tender.

~ Put half the mixture in a blender, together with half of the cream, and blend them together. Tip the purée into a bowl. Repeat for the remainder of the mixture, using the remainder of the cream. Season the creamy purée with the salt and pepper. Chill the soup, and sprinkle with chopped parsley before serving.

Curaçao

Sopito

Fish and Coconut Soup

SERVES 6

2 onions
1 garlic clove
2 bay leaves
1 celery stick, chopped
1 leek, chopped
1 tsp whole peppercorns
1 tbsp finely chopped fresh basil
1 tsp cumin seeds
1 tsp salt
5 cups cold water
1 lb whole fish (sea bream, red snapper, or mullet),
cleaned and scaled
¼ lb salt beef, diced
2 whole cloves
1 fresh hot pepper, sliced (see page 16)
1¼ cups coconut milk (see page 15)
3 tbsp cornmeal
½ lb unshelled shrimp
1 tbsp finely chopped fresh basil, to garnish

~Slice one of the onions, and put the slices in a saucepan with the garlic, bay leaves, celery, leek, peppercorns, basil, cumin seeds, and 1 teaspoon salt. Pour in the 5 cups cold water.

~Bring to the boil over a moderate heat, then lower the heat, cover, and simmer for 15 minutes.

~Add the fish and cook for 10 to 15 minutes, until the fish flakes easily when tested with a fork.

~Remove the pan from the heat, and sieve the stock into a clean pan. Reserve the fish.

~Finely chop the second onion and add it to the fish stock, together with the diced beef, cloves, hot pepper, and coconut milk.

~Bring to the boil over a moderate heat, then lower the heat, cover, and simmer for 45 minutes until the beef is tender, removing the hot pepper 15 minutes into this time and discarding it.

~Sprinkle the cornmeal over the stock mixture and cook for 2 minutes, stirring constantly.

~Skin and bone the fish, and cut the flesh into 1-inch pieces. Add the fish and shrimp to the soup, and cook over a low heat for 5 minutes.

~Serve in warmed soup bowls, garnished with the fresh, chopped basil.

29

Puerto Rico

Green Pigeon Pea Soup

SERVES 6

½ cup butter or margarine
1 medium onion, finely chopped
1 fat garlic clove, crushed
1 large, firm tomato, peeled, deseeded and chopped
1 small green pepper, deseeded, white pith removed, and
finely chopped
¼ lb cooked boned chicken, diced
1 lb fresh pumpkin, peeled, deseeded and diced

2½ cups chicken stock
1-lb can green pigeon peas with liquid
salt and freshly ground black pepper

~Melt the butter or margarine in a large saucepan, and fry the onion and garlic over a moderate heat until they are soft.

~Add the tomato, green pepper and chicken, cover the pan, and simmer for 5 minutes.

~Add the pumpkin, chicken stock, and green pigeon peas, and bring to the boil. Reduce the heat and simmer for 20 minutes, or until the soup thickens and the pumpkin is tender.

~The soup should be lumpy. Season to taste with salt and freshly ground black pepper, and serve at once.

Starters and Snacks

CHEESE CORN STICKS ~ Puerto Rico

STAMP AND GO ~ Jamaica

SHRIMP AND POTATO CAKES ~ Dominican Republic

BEEF PATTIES ~ Jamaica

OYSTER COCKTAIL ~ Grenada

CHICKEN AND RICE CROQUETTES ~ Antigua

PALM HEART SALAD ~ Martinique

ESCOVITCH ~ Barbados

BULJOL ~ Trinidad

Cheese Corn Sticks

Starters and Snacks

MAKES 24

2½ cups water
1 tsp salt
¾ cup yellow cornmeal
¾ cup Edam or cheddar, grated
vegetable oil for frying

~Bring the water, with the salt added, to the boil in a saucepan. Gradually add the cornmeal, stirring constantly. Continue to stir for 10 minutes, until the mixture is thick.

~Remove the saucepan from the heat. Add the grated cheese and mix it in well, then leave the mixture to cool.

~Wetting your hands in cold water from time to time, make the mixture into sticks about 3 inches long and 1 inch wide. Lay them on waxed paper, and chill for 3 hours or a day.

~When ready to fry, preheat the oven to its lowest temperature and line a baking dish with aluminum foil.

~Heat a little vegetable oil in a frying pan and fry 4 sticks at a time, turning them over and cooking them until they are crisp. Transfer the cooked sticks to the baking dish, and keep them warm in the oven while you fry the rest. Serve them hot.

32

Stamp and Go

Cod Fish-cakes

MAKES 24

¹/₂ lb salt cod
2 tbsp vegetable oil mixed with 1 tsp liquid annatto
(see page 14)
1 medium onion, finely chopped
1 cup flour
1 tsp baking powder
¹/₂ tsp salt
1 egg, lightly beaten
¹/₂ cup milk
2¹/₂ tsp melted butter or margarine
¹/₂ fresh hot pepper, finely chopped (see page 16)
vegetable oil for frying

~ Soak the salt cod in a glass bowl for 12 hours, changing the water 3 or 4 times during this time.

~ Drain the cod, rinse it under cold running water, and then put it into a large saucepan and cover with fresh cold water. Bring to the boil, then reduce the heat and simmer for 20 minutes.

~ Drain off the water, and lift out the fish. Remove the skin and bones, and flake the fish.

~ Heat the annatto-flavored oil in a clean large saucepan. Add the onion, and cook until soft.

~ Remove the pan from the heat, and set to one side.

~ Sift the flour, baking powder, and salt into a large mixing bowl. Add the egg, milk and melted butter or margarine, and mix together. Add the cooked onion and oil, the flaked cod, and the hot pepper. Mix together to form a batter.

~ Pour vegetable oil to a depth of ¹/₂ inch into a large frying pan, and heat until very hot. Drop the batter, a tablespoon at a time, into the hot oil, and fry for 3 minutes, turning the fish cakes over so they cook evenly. Drain on paper towels. These fish cakes can be eaten hot or cold.

33

Dominican Republic

Shrimp and Potato Cakes

MAKES 14

2 medium baking potatoes, peeled and quartered
1/3 cup butter or margarine
1 1/2 cups cheddar cheese, grated
1 egg yolk
3 tbsp finely chopped fresh parsley
1 tsp salt
freshly ground black pepper
1 medium onion, finely chopped
1 lb cooked shelled shrimp, deveined and chopped
1/2 cup flour
1 egg, lightly beaten
1/3 cup soft, fresh, white breadcrumbs
vegetable oil for frying

~ Boil the potatoes in salted water until they are soft.

~ Drain and mash the potatoes with a fork. Add two thirds of the butter or margarine, the cheese, egg yolk, parsley, salt, and freshly ground black pepper to taste. Mix well until the mixture is smooth.

~ Melt the remaining butter or margarine in a frying pan. Add the onion and cook for 5 minutes, then add the shrimp and cook for 1 minute.

~ Add the contents of the frying pan to the potato mixture and mix together well. Chill the mixture and form it into round shapes, approximately 1 1/2 inch in diameter, with your hands, and roll each one in flour and brush with the beaten egg. Dip each in the breadcrumbs, and put the finished cakes on waxed paper.

~ Deep fry 5 cakes at a time, turning them over when they are golden. Drain them on paper towels, and serve hot or cold.

34

Above Beach with palms, Anguilla.

Jamaica

Beef Patties

MAKES 12

FOR THE PASTRY
4 cups plain flour
2 tsp turmeric
1 tsp salt
1 cup butter, softened, or margarine
3 tbsp cold water

FOR THE FILLING
2 tbsp vegetable oil
1 onion, finely chopped
2 scallions, finely chopped
2 garlic cloves, crushed
2 fresh hot peppers, deseeded and finely chopped
¾ lb ground beef
4 tomatoes, skinned and chopped
¼ tsp turmeric
¼ tsp ground cumin
¼ tsp ground ginger

¼ tsp ground cinnamon
¼ tsp ground cloves
¼ ground cardamom
½ cup water
salt and freshly ground black pepper

FOR THE GLAZE
2 egg yolks, beaten

~ First make the pastry. Sift the flour, turmeric, and salt into a bowl. Add the butter or margarine, and mix well until the mixture resembles breadcrumbs. Mix in just enough of the cold water to form a stiff dough. Wrap the dough in plastic wrap, and chill for 2 hours.

~ For the filling, heat the oil in a medium saucepan and fry the onion until it is soft. Add the scallions, garlic and hot peppers, and cook for 2 more minutes.

~ Add the beef, tomatoes and spices, and season to taste with salt and freshly ground black pepper. Reduce the heat, stir in ½ cup water, and cook for 20 minutes.

~ Remove the pan from the heat, and leave the mixture to cool.

~ Meanwhile, preheat the oven to 400°F. Roll out the pastry, and cut out 12 circles approximately 7 inches in diameter using a saucer.

~ Put 2 tablespoons of the filling on one side of the circle, then fold the other half over so the edges meet. Crimp the edges together with a fork to seal. Place them on a baking tray lined with aluminum foil, and brush the tops with the beaten egg yolk glaze. Bake in the center of the oven for 30 minutes until golden brown. Serve at once.

37

Grenada

Oyster Cocktail

SERVES 6

24 fresh oysters
4 tsp lime juice
½ tsp hot pepper sauce
1 onion, finely chopped
2 tsp salt
1 small, fresh tomato, skinned and finely chopped
1 tsp olive oil

~ Rinse the oysters under cold running water, then leave them to soak in a bowl of cold water with 1 teaspoon of the lime juice for 5 minutes. Drain off the water.

~ In a bowl, mix the remaining lime juice with the hot pepper sauce, onion, salt, tomato, and olive oil. Add the oysters, and leave to marinate for 5 minutes.

~ Chill for 10 minutes before serving.

Left Beef Patties

Chicken and Rice Croquettes

MAKES 24

1 lb cooked, diced chicken
2½ cups cooked rice (about 2 cups uncooked)
½ onion, chopped
2 tsp tomato catsup
salt and freshly ground black pepper
½ tsp paprika
3 eggs, beaten
1 cup dried breadcrumbs
vegetable oil for frying

~ Mix all the ingredients together, except the eggs, breadcrumbs, and oil. Roll the mixture into small balls, then dip each one in the beaten egg and roll in the breadcrumbs to coat them.

~ Heat some oil in a saucepan and deep-fry the croquettes until they are golden brown. Serve at once with hot pepper sauce on the side.

Palm Heart Salad

SERVES 6

4-oz can palm hearts, drained
2 green mangoes, peeled and thinly sliced
½ cucumber, peeled and thinly sliced
2 ripe avocado pears
½ fresh hot pepper, deseeded and thinly sliced
(see page 16)

FOR THE DRESSING
juice of 1 lime or lemon
1 tsp mustard powder
1 tsp sugar
4 tbsp olive oil
salt and freshly ground black pepper

~ First make the dressing. Mix half the lime or lemon juice with the mustard powder, sugar, olive oil, salt, and freshly ground black pepper.

~ Next, make the salad. Chop the palm hearts into slices. Put the palm heart slices, mango, and cucumber into a glass serving bowl. Peel, stone, and thinly slice the avocados, and add them to the bowl. Stir in the hot pepper, together with the rest of the lime or lemon juice to prevent the ingredients discoloring.

~ Serve the salad with the dressing on the side.

Above Fishing boats, Martinique.

Right Palm Heart Salad.

Barbados

Escovitch

Pickled Fish

SERVES 6

*4 onions, thinly sliced
2 carrots, scraped and sliced
2 green peppers, deseeded and chopped
2 bay leaves
½ tsp fresh hot pepper, crushed (see page 16)
2 tsp salt
freshly ground black pepper
6 tbsp white wine vinegar
5 tbsp olive oil
1¼ cups cold water
2 lb red snapper, skinned and filleted*

~Put the onions, carrots, green peppers, bay leaves, hot pepper, salt and freshly ground black pepper to taste, plus the vinegar, 1½ tablespoons of the oil, and the water into a large saucepan, and bring to the boil over a high heat. Reduce the heat, and simmer until the vegetables are cooked.

~Meanwhile, pour the remaining oil into a large frying pan and heat. Add the fish fillets and cook each side for 2 minutes, or until golden brown. Transfer the fish to a shallow heatproof dish. Pour the contents of the saucepan over the fish, and leave to cool.

~Serve with baked yams or breadfruit.

Left *Escovitch.*

Trinidad

Buljol

Salt Cod Salad

SERVES 6

*½ lb salt cod, soaked overnight and drained
juice of 1 lime or lemon
1 onion, finely chopped
3 tomatoes, chopped
3 tbsp olive oil
2 hard-boiled eggs, chopped
1 fresh hot pepper, deseeded and finely chopped
(see page 16)
2 tbsp finely chopped scallions
1 green pepper, deseeded and finely chopped
2 tbsp finely chopped fresh parsley
freshly ground black pepper*

~Boil the cod for 20 minutes or until it flakes.

~Drain off the water, and rinse under cold running water. Remove the skin and bones, and flake the fish. Put the flaked fish into a glass bowl, add the lime or lemon juice, onion, tomatoes, olive oil, eggs, hot pepper, scallions, green pepper, parsley and freshly ground black pepper, and mix well.

~When the mixture has cooled, cover the bowl with plastic wrap and refrigerate overnight.

~Serve the next day on crackers, fresh bread, or small, toasted slices of bread.

Chicken Dishes

CARIB-ORIENT CHICKEN ~ Guyana

CALYPSO CHICKEN ~ Jamaica

MARINATED FRIED CHICKEN ~ Dominican Republic

CHICKEN AND RICE STEW ~ Puerto Rico

POULET ROTI à LA CRÉOLE ~ Haiti

CORIANDER CHICKEN ~ Trinidad

CHICKEN AND NOODLE BAKE ~ Guyana

SWEET AND SPICY CHICKEN ~ Grenada

POULET AU JARDINIÈRE ~ Guadeloupe

Guyana

Carib-Orient Chicken

SERVES 4

3 lb chicken, cut into 2-in pieces
½ cup soy sauce
2 tbsp brown sugar
2 garlic cloves, crushed
1 tbsp grated fresh ginger root
3 tbsp white wine

~ Wash the chicken pieces and put them in a bowl.

~ Combine the remaining ingredients in a large saucepan and stir over a medium heat until the sugar has dissolved. Leave to cool.

~ Pour the sauce over the chicken and leave to marinate for 5 hours.

44

~ Grill the chicken pieces until they are tender and serve.

Jamaica

Calypso Chicken

SERVES 6

3 lb chicken, cut into 2-in pieces
½ lemon
2 tsp salt
freshly ground black pepper
2 garlic cloves
1 tbsp vinegar
¼ tsp chopped fresh thyme
2 tbsp butter or margarine
2 tsp brown sugar
oil for frying
1 cup cashew nuts
¼ lb mushrooms, sliced
3 onions, chopped
6 slices fresh root ginger
1 tbsp plain flour

~ Wash the chicken in cold running water, rubbing with the lemon. Season with the salt, pepper, one of the cloves of garlic, crushed, plus the vinegar and thyme. Leave to marinate for about 3 hours.

~ In a large saucepan, melt the butter or margarine, then add the sugar. When it is bubbling, add the chicken and brown the pieces.

~ Meanwhile, in a frying pan, heat some oil. Fry half the cashews, then set them aside. In the same pan, fry together the remaining clove of garlic, crushed, the mushrooms, the other half of the cashews, onions and ginger. Add ¼ cup water, and pour the mixture into the large saucepan over the chicken. Cook for 25 minutes or until the chicken is cooked.

~ Thicken with the flour mixed with some warm water and stirred into the chicken mixture. Cook for 3 more minutes, then sprinkle with the remaining fried cashews.

~ Serve with boiled rice.

Right *Calypso Chicken.*

Dominican Republic

Marinated Fried Chicken

SERVES 4

3 tbsp dark rum
3 tbsp soy sauce
3 tbsp lime juice
4 lb chicken, cut into 16 pieces
1 garlic clove, crushed
1/2 tsp salt
freshly ground black pepper
1 cup plain flour
vegetable oil for deep frying

~Warm the rum in a small pan over a low heat. Remove the pan from the heat, and set light to the rum with a match. Shake the pan backwards and forwards until the flame dies. Add the soy sauce and lime juice to the rum. Put the chicken pieces in a bowl, and pour the rum mixture over them. Add the garlic, mix it in well, then leave to marinate for 4 hours, turning the pieces now and then.

~Preheat the oven to its lowest temperature, and line a heatproof dish with aluminum foil.

~Heat some oil in a big frying pan. Pat the chicken pieces dry with paper towels, and then season with the salt and freshly ground black pepper. Dip the pieces in the flour, shaking them to remove any excess, and then fry them. When the pieces are golden brown, transfer them to the prepared dish and keep them warm in the oven.

~Serve with hot boiled rice and a mixed vegetable stew.

Puerto Rico

Chicken and Rice Stew

SERVES 6

1 garlic clove, chopped
1/2 tsp dried oregano
1/2 tsp salt
3 lb chicken, cut into 8 pieces
1/4 cup butter or margarine
1 small onion, finely chopped
2/3 cup green peppers, chopped
4 ripe tomatoes, skinned and chopped
1 1/2 cups uncooked long-grain white rice
3 3/4 pints chicken stock
freshly ground black pepper
2 1/4 cups frozen peas
1/4 cup Parmesan cheese, freshly grated
1 fresh hot pepper, chopped (see page 16)

~Mix the garlic, oregano, and salt together in a large bowl. Add the chicken pieces, and mix them well together. Heat the butter or margarine in a saucepan, and brown the chicken pieces. Transfer them to a plate.

~Add the onion and green peppers to the pan, and cook until soft.

~Add the tomatoes and browned chicken pieces, coating them well with the onion, peppers, and tomato mixture. Reduce the heat and simmer for 30 minutes, or until the chicken is cooked.

~Remove the chicken to a plate and leave to cool a little.

~Remove the bones, and cut the flesh into 2-inch pieces.

~Meanwhile, add the rice, stock and freshly ground black pepper to the onion, peppers and tomato mixture, and bring to the boil. Reduce the heat, cover, and simmer for 20 minutes or until the rice is cooked.

~Stir in the peas, Parmesan, and hot pepper. Mix well, then add the chicken. Cover and simmer for 2 more minutes, then serve.

Poulet Roti à la Créole

Roast Chicken Creole-style

SERVES 6

½ cup butter or margarine
1 small clove garlic, peeled
6 tbsp soft, fresh breadcrumbs
3 tbsp lime juice
2 tsp finely grated lime rind
4 tbsp dark rum
1 tsp brown sugar
¼ tsp ground cinnamon
¼ tsp cayenne pepper
1 tsp salt
freshly ground black pepper
3 ripe bananas
4 lb whole roasting chicken, turkey, or goose
1¼ cups chicken stock

48

~Preheat oven to 350°F.

~Melt half the butter or margarine in a small frying pan, then add the garlic and stir it around the pan for 10 seconds. Remove and discard the garlic. Add the breadcrumbs, two-thirds of the lime juice, the lime rind, a quarter of the rum, the sugar, cinnamon, cayenne pepper, salt and freshly ground black pepper to taste. Mix well, and set the stuffing on one side.

~Peel and chop the bananas, then put them in a bowl. Add the remaining lime juice, 2 tbsp rum, and salt and freshly ground black pepper to taste. Mix well together. Stuff the chicken or other fowl with the banana stuffing, and sew the opening closed with a large needle and trussing string.

~Fill the small neck cavity with the breadcrumb stuffing, and sew up the opening in the same way as before.

~Brush the chicken with the remaining butter or margarine. Place it in a roasting pan, and roast in the preheated oven for 1 hour, basting occasionally with the juices.

~After removing the chicken from the oven, transfer it to a large heated dish and leave it to rest for 5 minutes, as this makes it easier to carve. Meanwhile, skim the fat from the juices left in the roasting pan, and pour in the chicken stock. Bring to the boil over a high heat, stirring all the time. Cook for 2 minutes, taste for seasoning, and pour into a sauceboat.

~Just before serving, warm the last tablespoon of rum in a small pan. Remove it from the heat, then set light to the rum with a match and pour it, flaming, over the chicken. Serve immediately.

Trinidad

Coriander Chicken

SERVES 4

3 lb chicken, cut into 2-in pieces
1 tsp salt
1/2 tsp freshly ground black pepper
3 garlic cloves
2 tsp lemon juice
2 tbsp ground coriander
1 small bunch fresh coriander
3 tbsp butter or margarine

~Season the chicken with the salt, pepper, garlic, lemon juice, and half the ground coriander. Chop the fresh coriander finely and mix it in with the chicken, then leave to marinate for 4 hours.

~Preheat the oven to 350°F.

~Drain the chicken. Melt the butter or margarine. Place the chicken in a heatproof dish, and pour the melted butter or margarine over the chicken. Sprinkle with the remaining ground coriander, then bake in the preheated oven for 1 hour or until the chicken is cooked.

~Just before serving, grill the chicken to brown it.

~Serve with rice and salad.

Guyana

Chicken and Noodle Bake

SERVES 4

6 chicken legs
1 tsp salt
freshly ground black pepper
1 garlic clove, crushed
2 tbsp butter or margarine
1 onion, chopped
1 × 10-oz can condensed cream of mushroom soup
1/2 cup milk
1/2 lb dried noodles
1 1/2 cups cheese, grated
1 tbsp chopped fresh parsley

~Season the chicken legs with the salt, pepper, and garlic. Leave them to marinate for approximately 4 hours.

~Melt the butter or margarine in a large saucepan. Add the onion, and cook until soft.

~Drain the chicken legs, add them to the pan, and brown them on all sides. Stir in the mushroom soup and milk, cover, and simmer for 30 minutes.

~Preheat the oven to 400°F.

~Cook the noodles as given in the instructions on the packet, then drain them and rinse in cold water. Place them in a greased heatproof dish. Arrange the chicken legs on top of the noodles, pour the sauce over, and sprinkle with the cheese and parsley. Bake in the preheated oven for 30 minutes.

51

Left *Coriander Chicken.*

Grenada

Sweet and Spicy Chicken

Guadeloupe

Poulet au Jardinière

Chicken Casserole

52

SERVES 6

3 lb chicken, cut into 2-in pieces
2 tbsp olive oil
1 onion, finely chopped
2 scallions, finely chopped
2 garlic cloves, crushed
1 fresh hot pepper, chopped (see page 16)
1/2 tsp brown sugar
1 tsp thyme
1 tsp basil
1 christophene, peeled, deseeded, and chopped
1 eggplant, peeled and cubed
1/4 lb okra, trimmed and chopped
14-oz can tomatoes, drained and chopped
salt and freshly ground black pepper

~Wash the chicken pieces.

~Heat the oil in a large saucepan, and add the onion, scallions, and garlic. Cook over a low heat for 5 minutes.

~Add the chicken pieces, and cook for 5 minutes to brown them.

~Stir in the hot pepper, sugar, herbs and vegetables, and season to taste with salt and freshly ground black pepper. Pour in 1 1/4 cups cold water and bring to the boil, then lower the heat and, stirring occasionally, simmer uncovered for 1 hour or until the chicken and vegetables are cooked and the sauce has thickened.

~Serve with fresh bread, baked yams, or boiled rice.

SERVES 6

3 lb chicken, cut into 2-in pieces
1 tsp salt
1 tsp freshly ground black pepper
2 garlic cloves
1/4 tsp chopped fresh thyme
2 tsp vinegar
1 bay leaf
2 tbsp vegetable oil
1 medium tomato, chopped
1 onion, finely chopped
2 celery sticks, chopped
2 carrots, diced
1/4 cabbage, shredded
4 potatoes, chopped
6 oz green beans, cleaned

~Wash the chicken. Marinate the pieces in a bowl with the salt, pepper, garlic, thyme, bay leaf, and vinegar for 5 hours.

~Heat the oil in a large saucepan, then add the tomatoes and chicken pieces. Cover with cold water, bring it to the boil, then lower the heat and simmer, covered, for 30 minutes or until the chicken is almost cooked and the liquid has reduced.

~Add the onion and the other vegetables, and cook until they are tender but crisp.

~Serve immediately with fresh bread or boiled rice and hot pepper sauce.

Meat Dishes

ROAST PORK CALYPSO ~ Jamaica

BAKED PAPAYA WITH MEAT FILLING ~ Jamaica

PEPPERPOT ~ Guyana

CURRIED MEATBALLS ~ Surinam

RABBIT IN PIMENTO SAUCE ~ Puerto Rico

BEEF STEAKS À L'OIGNON ~ Guadeloupe

BRAISED LAMB ~ Puerto Rico

LAMB AND SALT BEEF STEW ~ Curaçao

GROUND BEEF SPECIAL ~ Barbados

BEEF WITH BEANSPROUTS ~ Trinidad

Jamaica

Roast Pork Calypso

SERVES 6

4 lb piece of pork
2 cups cold water
1 tbsp vinegar
1 tbsp salt
3 garlic cloves, crushed
1 tsp thyme
1 onion, grated
1 tsp ground cloves
1 tbsp chopped fresh parsley

~Place the pork in a large saucepan, cover with the cold water, and add the vinegar, salt, garlic, and thyme. Leave to marinate for several hours.

~Meanwhile, mix the onion, cloves, and parsley in a bowl.

~Preheat the oven to 325°F.

~When the pork is ready, remove it from the saucepan and make 2-inch long gashes all over. Fill the holes with the onion mixture. Pour the marinade into a baking dish. Lay the pork in the dish, and roast in the preheated oven for 30 minutes until it is done.

Left *Roast Pork Calypso.*

Jamaica

Baked Papaya with Meat Filling

SERVES 6

2 tbsp vegetable oil
1 small onion, finely chopped
1 garlic clove, crushed
1 lb lean ground beef or lamb
4 ripe tomatoes, skinned and chopped
2 chilies for a hot dish, or ½ thinly chopped fresh hot pepper for a mild flavor
1 tsp salt
freshly ground black pepper
5 lb green papaya, halved and deseeded
½ cup cheese, grated

~Preheat the oven to 350°F.

~Heat the oil in a large frying pan, and fry the onion and garlic in it for 5 minutes. Then, stir in the beef or lamb and cook until browned.

~Add the tomatoes, chilies or hot pepper, salt, and freshly ground black pepper to taste. Continue to cook until all the liquid has evaporated.

~Spoon the meat mixture into the papaya shells, and place them in a shallow roasting pan. Pour in enough boiling water around them to reach approximately 1 inch up the sides of the shells when they are placed side by side. Bake in the preheated oven for 1 hour.

~Sprinkle with half the grated cheese and bake for another 30 minutes.

~Serve sprinkled with the remaining grated cheese.

57

Guyana

Pepperpot

SERVES 6

¼ cup vegetable oil

3 lb fresh, lean pork, chopped

1 lb salt pork, chopped

3¾ cups cold water

2 large onions, chopped

1 bunch thyme, chopped

3 garlic cloves, crushed

2 tbsp brown sugar

½ cup cassareep (see page 15)

4 hot peppers

~ Heat the oil in a large saucepan and fry the meat. Cover with the cold water, then add the onions, thyme, garlic, sugar, and cassareep. Tie the chilies in a clean cloth and set aside. Simmer the meat, covered, for 4 hours until it is cooked. Add the cloth containing the hot peppers and simmer for 15 minutes. Remove the pan from the heat and serve hot.

~ Pepperpot can be kept at room temperature for 3 days – the chilies and spices act as preservatives – and reheated when necessary.

Curried Meatballs

MAKES 12

1 tbsp butter or margarine
1 onion, chopped
1 lb lean ground beef
2 tsp salt
1 tsp lemon juice
1 tsp chili powder
1 tsp ground coriander
1 tbsp vegetable oil
1 medium onion, grated
1 garlic clove, crushed
pinch ground cloves
1 tsp turmeric
1 tsp sugar
4 tomatoes, chopped

~Melt the butter or margarine in a medium-sized saucepan and add the chopped onion. Fry it for 1–2 minutes, then add the beef, salt, lemon juice, chili powder, and coriander. Remove the pan from the heat and shape the beef mixture into balls.

~Heat the oil in the saucepan and add the grated onion, garlic, cloves, turmeric, sugar, and tomatoes. Simmer for 15 minutes.

~Add the meatballs, and cook for 15 more minutes.

~Serve hot with steamed rice.

59

Puerto Rico

Rabbit in Pimento Sauce

SERVES 4

2 lb rabbit, chopped into 2-in pieces
1 tsp salt
freshly ground black pepper
1/4 cup butter or margarine
1 medium onion, chopped
1 fat garlic clove, chopped
2 tbsp brandy
2 tbsp sherry
3 ripe tomatoes, skinned and chopped
1/2 fresh hot pepper, chopped (see page 16)
1/3 cup drained pimentos, finely chopped
2/3 cup chicken stock
1 bay leaf
1/2 tsp sugar

~Preheat the oven to 350°F.

~Season the rabbit pieces with the salt and freshly ground black pepper to taste. Heat the butter or margarine in a large casserole dish and brown the rabbit. Transfer the rabbit to a dish and put to one side.

~Add the onions and garlic to the casserole, cook them for 5 minutes, then pour them over the rabbit.

~Pour the brandy into the casserole and heat it. Remove the casserole from the heat, and set light to the brandy with a match. Shake the casserole backwards and forwards until the flame dies. Add the sherry to the brandy in the casserole and bring to the boil. Add the tomatoes, hot pepper, pimentos, chicken stock, bay leaf and sugar, and season to taste with freshly ground black pepper. Add the rabbit, bring to the boil, and cook for 30 minutes.

~Remove the casserole from the heat, cover, and bake in the preheated oven for 2 hours.

~Serve with rice.

61

Guadeloupe

Beef Steaks à l'Oignon

Steaks with Onions

SERVES 6

6 very thin beef steaks
2 garlic cloves, crushed
2 tsp salt
freshly ground black pepper
1 tsp vinegar
1/4 cup butter or margarine
1 onion, sliced
2 tsp brandy

~Season the steaks with the garlic, salt, pepper and vinegar, then leave them to stand for 3 hours.

~In a large frying pan, heat the butter or margarine. Fry the steaks quickly to brown them on both sides, then remove them to a warm plate.

~Add the onion to the frying pan, and fry for 2 minutes.

~Add the brandy to the pan, heat through, then pour the onion and brandy over the steaks and serve immediately.

~Serve with a green salad and baked sweet potatoes.

Left Rabbit in Pimento Sauce.

Puerto Rico

Braised Lamb

SERVES 6

6 lamb chops
3 tbsp honey
2 tbsp dry sherry
¼ cup soy sauce
2 tbsp white vinegar
2 garlic cloves, crushed
¼ cup chicken stock
2 tsp brown sugar
2 tbsp dark rum

~ Place the lamb chops in a glass bowl. Mix all the remaining ingredients together and pour over the chops. Refrigerate overnight.

~ Put the chops and marinade in an ovenproof dish, and cover with foil or a lid. Bake at 350°F for 45 minutes, then serve at once.

~ Serve with baked cassava or breadfruit.

Curaçao

Lamb and Salt Beef Stew

SERVES 6

½ lb lean salt beef
¼ cup butter or margarine
1 tbsp vegetable oil
2 lb boned lamb or goat cut into 1-in pieces
2 onions, finely chopped
1 large tomato, skinned and chopped
2 tsp peeled and chopped fresh root ginger
¼ green pepper, chopped
1 fat garlic clove, chopped
½ fresh hot pepper, chopped (see page 16)
1 tsp salt
2 tsp ground cumin
2 tbsp lime or lemon juice
2½ cups water
3 potatoes, peeled and diced
2 cucumbers, peeled and diced

~ Put the salt beef in a saucepan, cover with cold water, bring to the boil, and then boil for 30 minutes.

~ Drain the meat and cut it into cubes.

~ Heat the butter or margarine and oil in a large saucepan, then add the lamb or goat and brown it all over. Remove the meat and set to one side.

~ Add the onions to the saucepan and cook for 5 minutes. Then add the tomato, ginger, green pepper, garlic, hot pepper, salt, and cumin. Cook for 10 minutes, stirring constantly.

~ Stir in the prepared salt beef, lamb, lime or lemon juice, and 2½ cups of water. Cook for 1 hour over low heat.

~ Add the potatoes and cucumber, and simmer for 20 more minutes.

Barbados

Ground Beef Special

Trinidad

Beef with Beansprouts

SERVES 6

2 lb ground beef
1 tsp salt
freshly ground black pepper
$1/2$ tsp thyme
2 scallions, chopped
1 lb chestnuts
$1/4$ cup olive oil
1 large onion, chopped
2 garlic cloves, crushed
$3^3/4$ cups water
1 tsp chopped fresh basil
3 cups rice
$1/2$ cup cashew nuts, chopped

~Season the ground beef with the salt, pepper, thyme and scallions, and leave to infuse for 1 hour.

~Cook the chestnuts in boiling water until they are soft, and shell them once they are cool enough to handle.

~In a saucepan, heat the oil, then add the onion and garlic and cook for 5 minutes over a medium heat. Add the ground beef, and cook until it has lightly browned all over. Add $3^3/4$ cups of cold water and the basil, and simmer.

~Meanwhile, wash the rice and drain it well. Add the rice to the beef mixture, and cook until the rice is tender and the water has been absorbed. Sprinkle the cashews over the top.

~Serve hot with a green salad.

SERVES 4

1 lb lean beef, cut into tiny pieces
$1/2$ tsp salt
freshly ground black pepper
1 garlic clove, crushed
1 tbsp vegetable oil
1 tbsp soy sauce
1 medium onion, chopped
2 tbsp beef stock
$1/2$ cup fresh beansprouts

~Season the beef with the salt, garlic, and freshly ground black pepper to taste.

~Heat the oil in a frying pan, then add the soy sauce. Fry the beef until it is evenly browned, then add the onions and stock. Cook for 5 minutes, stirring all the time, then lower the heat, add the beansprouts, and cook for 10 more minutes.

~Serve with steamed rice and hot pepper sauce.

Above *Coconut palms, Trinidad.*

Right *Beef with Beansprouts.*

Fish and Seafood Dishes

BAKED LOBSTER ~ Jamaica

LOBSTER IN CHILI SAUCE ~ Cuba

BLAFF ~ Martinique

FRIED FLYING FISH ~ Barbados

COURT BOUILLON à LA CRÉOLE ~ Martinique

RICE WITH SHRIMP AND TOMATOES ~ Dominica

BAKED EDAM CHEESE WITH SHRIMP STUFFING ~ Curaçao

CRABS IN PEPPER SAUCE ~ Dominican Republic

CRAB GUMBO ~ Antigua

BAKED FISH WITH ONIONS ~ Cuba

68

Fish Tips

The Caribbean waters are rich in fish and seafood. Typical Caribbean fish are grouper, kingfish, Spanish mackerel, snappers, flying fish (a fish with "wings" that are, in fact, extended fins, found off the coasts of Barbados), and dolphin fish — no relation to the mammal.

~ Some Caribbean fish have bizarre shapes: the coffer fish is square-shaped and the moonfish is round and silvery, for example. The people of Martinique have named a fish "bon-die marie moin," which is Creole meaning "good God handled me," for this fish has unearthly fingerprints along its sides.

~ The Caribbean waters also contain plenty of crabs, shrimp, octopus, spiny lobsters, conch (called lambi), which are enormous sea snails with big horns, and sea eggs, a kind of white sea urchin without spines.

~ When you buy fish, make sure that it is fresh. Signs of this are eyes that are clear and bright (avoid those with sunken eyes), skin that is shiny and moist, flesh that is firm, and a sea-fresh smell. Frozen fish should be frozen hard, with no sign of partial thawing.

~ When buying shellfish, make sure the shells are undamaged, with no cracks.

~ Most fish vendors will clean, bone, and fillet fish for you. Nowadays many exotic fish are on display at seafood shops and in supermarkets, including mackerel, jacks or trevally, kingfish, snapper, swordfish, tuna, sea bream, parrotfish, and pomfrets. Octopus, squid, shrimp, crabs, and lobster are also available.

Jamaica

Baked Lobster

SERVES 4

2 lb cooked lobster meat, cubed
2 tsp salt
1 garlic clove, crushed
1/4 tsp nutmeg
freshly ground black pepper
1/4 cup butter or margarine
3 3/4 cups light cream or evaporated milk
1 tsp hot pepper sauce
1/2 small onion, finely chopped
2 egg yolks
1 1/2 cups cheese, grated

~ Put the lobster into a bowl and stir in the salt, garlic, nutmeg, and freshly ground black pepper. Chill it for 1 hour.

~ Preheat the oven to 350°F.

~ Melt the butter or margarine in a large saucepan over a low heat. Gradually add the cream or evaporated milk, stirring all the time. Add the lobster, hot pepper sauce and onion, mixing them in well. Beat the egg yolks slightly, then add them to the saucepan.

~ Spoon the lobster mixture into a greased baking dish. Sprinkle half the grated cheese over the top, and bake in the preheated oven for 5 minutes.

~ Sprinkle with the remaining cheese just before serving.

~ Serve on a bed of rice or with mashed sweet potatoes.

Cuba

Lobster in Chili Sauce

SERVES 2

2 × 2 lb uncooked lobsters, split in half lengthways
2 tbsp vegetable oil mixed with 1 tsp liquid annatto (see page 14)
1 1/4 cups dry white wine
1 tsp salt
1/2 hot pepper, finely chopped (see page 16)

~ Remove and discard the gelatinous sac in the head of each lobster and the long intestinal vein attached to it. Chop off the tail section of each lobster at the point where it joins the body. Twist off the claws, and smash the flat side of each claw with a large, heavy knife. Cut off and discard the small claws and antennae.

~ Heat the oil in a large frying pan. Add the lobster bodies, tails, and large claws and fry them, stirring constantly, until the shells turn pink. Transfer the lobsters to a large plate.

~ Add the wine to the frying pan, and bring it to the boil. Stir in the salt and hot pepper. Return the lobsters to the pan, coat them evenly in the liquid, and cook for 10 minutes, basting them from time to time.

~ To serve, arrange the lobster pieces in a large, heated dish and spoon the sauce over them.

***Right** Lobster in Chili Sauce.*

Martinique

Blaff

Poached Marinated Fish

SERVES 2

5 cups water
6 tbsp fresh lime or lemon juice
2 tsp salt
2 × 1-lb fish, scaled, cleaned and cut into four fish
steaks about 1-in thick (snapper, sea bream,
jack, or mullet)
1 small onion, finely chopped
1 tsp crushed garlic cloves
1 hot pepper, chopped (see page 16)
2 bay leaves
1/2 tsp thyme

~Put half the water, half the lime or lemon juice, and salt into a large, shallow, glass baking dish. Wash the fish steaks under cold running water, then put them in the baking dish and leave to marinate for about 1 hour.

~Drain and discard the marinade.

~Pour the remaining water into a frying pan, together with the onion, garlic, hot pepper, bay leaves, and thyme. Bring to the boil over a high heat, then lower the heat and simmer for 5 minutes.

~Add the fish steaks to the pan, and bring back to the boil. Reduce the heat to the lowest setting, cover the pan, and simmer for 10 minutes or until the fish is cooked. Transfer the fish to a warmed serving dish. Add the remaining lime or lemon juice to the cooking liquid, and pour this over the fish. Taste to check the seasoning, then serve at once.

~Serve with fresh bread.

Barbados

Fried Flying Fish

SERVES 6

6 small, boned flying fish
1 tbsp lime or lemon juice
1 garlic clove, crushed
salt and freshly ground black pepper
1 tsp chopped fresh thyme
2 whole cloves
2 tsp plain flour
vegetable oil for frying

~Marinate the fish in the lemon or lime juice, garlic, salt and freshly ground black pepper, thyme and cloves for at least 1 hour.

~Remove the fish from the marinade, and dry them well with kitchen towels.

~Mix the flour with freshly ground black pepper, then coat the fish in it, shaking off any excess.

~Heat some oil (enough to cover the fish) in a big frying pan. Fry the fish until they are golden brown, then serve.

~Serve hot with rice and peas, salad, and hot pepper sauce.

71

Martinique

Court Bouillon à la Créole

Braised Marinated Fish Creole Style

SERVES 4

2¹/₂ cups water
6 tbsp fresh lime or lemon juice
2 tsp salt
2 lb firm fish (such as snapper or mullet), scaled,
cleaned, and cut into 4 × ¹/₂-lb steaks
3 tbsp vegetable oil mixed with 1 tsp liquid annatto
(see page 14)
4 scallions, chopped
4 garlic cloves, chopped
¹/₂ hot pepper, finely chopped (see page 16)
3 ripe tomatoes, skinned and chopped
1 tsp thyme
1 bay leaf
4 parsley sprigs
freshly ground black pepper
2 tbsp olive oil

~ Put 2 cups water, the lime or lemon juice and salt into a large, shallow, glass dish, and stir until the salt dissolves. Wash the fish steaks under cold running water, and marinate them in the lime or lemon juice mixture for 1 hour.

~ Remove the fish from the marinade. Heat the annatto-flavored oil in a large saucepan over a medium heat. Add the scallions, garlic and hot pepper, and cook until soft.

~ Add the tomatoes, thyme, bay leaf, parsley and freshly ground black pepper, and simmer for 10 minutes.

~ Stir in the remaining water, add the fish, and bring to the boil. Reduce the heat, and simmer for 10 more minutes.

~ Transfer the fish and sauce to a heated baking dish. Sprinkle with the olive oil, and bake in a preheated oven for 5 minutes.

Above *Codfish – salted cod is a Caribbean specialty.*

Dominica

Rice with Shrimp and Tomatoes

SERVES 4

2 tbsp olive oil
1 garlic clove, crushed
2 tomatoes, peeled and chopped
1 tsp saffron
2 tsp salt
1 tsp paprika
2 cups peas
1½ cups uncooked rice
freshly ground black pepper
2½ cups water
8 shrimp, cooked, shelled and deveined
12 scampi, cooked, shelled and deveined

~ Heat the oil in a saucepan, then fry the garlic in it for 2 minutes.

~ Add the tomatoes, saffron, salt, paprika, peas, rice, and freshly ground black pepper and fry for 5 minutes, then add the water.

~ Add the prawns and scampi and cook for 15 more minutes, or until the rice has cooked (if necessary adding some more water). Serve immediately.

~ Serve with a cucumber salad.

Curaçao

Baked Edam Cheese with Shrimp Stuffing

SERVES 6

4 lb whole Edam cheese
¼ cup butter or margarine
2 tsp vegetable oil
1 tbsp onion, finely chopped
1 tomato, skinned and chopped
¼ tsp chili powder
½ tsp salt
freshly ground black pepper
¾ lb cooked shrimp, shelled, deveined and chopped
3 tbsp soft, fresh, white breadcrumbs
1 egg, well beaten
2 tbsp raisins

~ Peel the wax off the cheese, and cut a 1-inch thick slice off the top and reserve. Scoop out the center of the cheese with a spoon to leave a shell 1 inch thick, reserving the scooped out cheese.

~ Place both the shell and top in enough cold water to cover them, and leave them to soak for 1 hour.

~ Remove the cheese shell and top from the water, turn them upside down, and leave them on paper towels to drain.

~ Grate the cheese removed from the center.

~ Preheat the oven to 350°F.

~ Grease a round baking dish with half the butter or margarine (it has to be large enough to hold the cheese shell – not too shallow or too large, but about the same size as the cheese shell itself).

~ Heat the remaining butter or margarine and vegetable oil in a frying pan over a medium heat. Add the onion and cook for 5 minutes, not letting it burn.

~ Add the tomato, chili powder, salt, and a few grindings of black pepper. Continue to cook until the mixture becomes thick, then transfer it to a bowl. Add the grated cheese, shrimp, breadcrumbs, egg, and raisins. Spoon the mixture into the cheese shell, cover with the cheese top, and put it in the prepared baking dish. Bake it in the preheated oven, uncovered, for 30 minutes until the top has browned slightly.

~ Serve at once, straight from the baking dish.

75

Left *Rice with Shrimp and Tomatoes.*

Dominican Republic

Crabs in Pepper Sauce

Antigua

Crab Gumbo

SERVES 6

3 tbsp olive oil
1 hot pepper, finely chopped
1 medium onion, finely chopped
½ green pepper, finely chopped
2 garlic cloves, finely chopped
6 ripe tomatoes, skinned and chopped
3 tbsp tomato purée
1 tsp salt
freshly ground black pepper
1 lb fresh, canned, or frozen crabmeat
2 tbsp fresh lime or lemon juice
2 tbsp finely chopped fresh coriander

~ Heat the oil in a large frying pan over a medium heat. Add the hot pepper, onion, green pepper, and garlic and fry for 5 minutes.

~ Add the tomatoes, tomato purée, salt, and freshly ground black pepper to taste. Bring the mixture to the boil, then lower the heat and cook, uncovered, until it has reduced to a thick sauce.

~ Add the crabmeat and stir it in. Simmer for 2 minutes.

~ Serve sprinkled with the lime or lemon juice and chopped coriander.

SERVES 6

2 × 2 lb cooked crabs
2 tbsp butter or margarine
1 tbsp vegetable oil
1 onion, chopped
14-oz can tomatoes, drained and chopped
1 tbsp chopped fresh thyme
2 tbsp chopped fresh parsley
½ lb okra, trimmed and sliced
1 fresh hot pepper
2½ cups boiling water
salt and freshly ground black pepper

~ Cut the legs and claws off the crabs, and crack them using a nutcracker. Cut the body into quarters.

~ Heat the butter or margarine and oil in a large saucepan over a medium heat. Add the onion and fry for 5 minutes.

~ Add the crabs and cook, turning the pieces over frequently.

~ Stir in the tomatoes, thyme and parsley, and cook for 5 more minutes.

~ Add the okra and hot pepper, and pour in 2½ cups boiling water. Season with salt and freshly ground black pepper, then lower the heat and simmer for 45 minutes.

~ Discard the hot pepper, and spoon the stew into warmed soup bowls.

~ Serve with fresh bread.

Right *Crab Gumbo.*

Cuba

Baked Fish with Onions

SERVES 6

2 lb red snappers or similar fish
salt and freshly ground black pepper
2 garlic cloves, crushed
juice of 1 lemon
1 cup water
1 large onion, finely chopped
6 tbsp fresh breadcrumbs
½ cup olive oil
1 tbsp chopped fresh parsley

~Clean, wash, and prepare the fish. Make an incision along the belly of each fish. Lightly sprinkle salt and freshly ground black pepper and some garlic both inside and outside. Rub lemon juice over the fish. Place in a pan, pour the water over the fish, and leave to marinate for at least an hour, preferably four.

~Preheat the oven to 350°F.

~Cook half the onion, the remaining garlic, and half the breadcrumbs in 1 tablespoon of the oil. Add a little water to make the mixture form a slightly crumbly texture, and leave it to cool.

~Stuff the fish with the onion and breadcrumbs mixture, then lay them in a greased baking dish and cover with the rest of the oil. Sprinkle the rest of the onion and breadcrumbs and the parsley over them. Bake them in the preheated oven for 30 minutes.

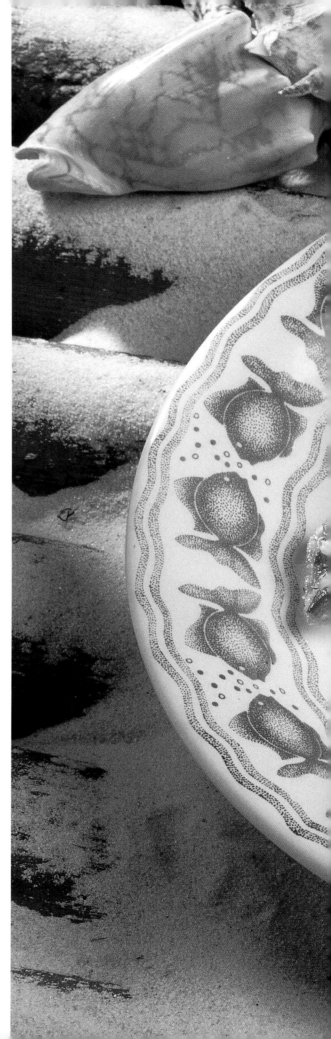

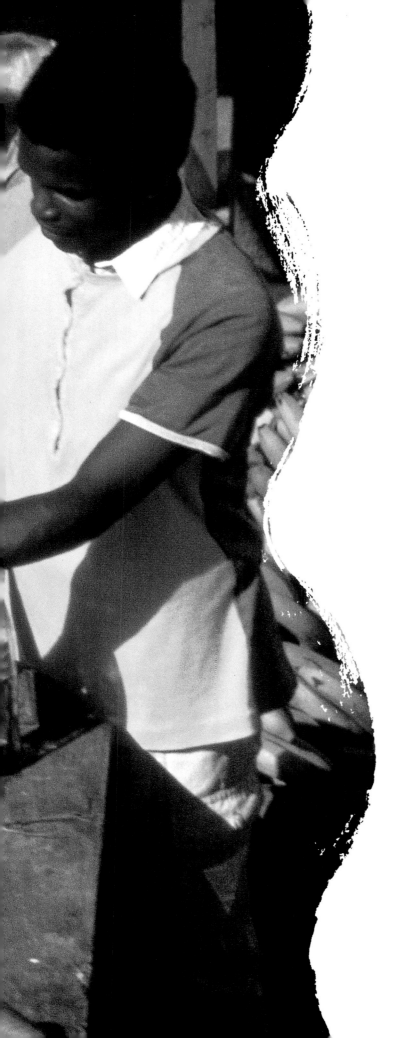

Vegetables and Pulses

GREEN PLANTAIN CHIPS ~ Jamaica

STEWED OKRAS ~ Puerto Rico

PIONONOS ~ Puerto Rico

BLACK BEANS AND RICE ~ Cuba

EGGPLANTS IN COCONUT SAUCE ~ Martinique

SWEET POTATO AND WALNUT SOUFFLÉ ~ Antigua

YAM SOUFFLÉ ~ Barbados

ACKEE AND SALT FISH ~ Jamaica

JUG JUG ~ Barbados

BAKED CHRISTOPHENE ~ Martinique

Green Plantain Chips

SERVES 6

4 green plantains
juice of ½ lime
salt
vegetable oil for deep frying

~Peel the plantains (see page 17) and rub them with the lime juice. Cut them into thin slices and mix well with a pinch of salt.

~Heat some oil in a large frying pan. Drain the plantain slices, then fry them for 3 minutes until they are crisp and golden brown.

~Remove them from the pan as soon as they are ready and drain them on paper towels.

~Serve when cool.

Stewed Okra

SERVES 6

2 lb fresh okra
2 tbsp butter or margarine
1 medium to large onion, finely chopped
1 garlic clove, crushed
8 ripe tomatoes, skinned and chopped
½ hot pepper, chopped (see page 16)
1 tsp salt

~Wash the okra under cold running water. Cut ½ inch off the stalk, at the narrow end.

~Melt the butter or margarine in a large saucepan over a medium heat. Add the onions and garlic, and fry until they are soft.

~Add the tomatoes and hot pepper, and cook for 5 more minutes.

~Add the okra and salt, stir, then reduce the heat. Cook for 20 more minutes, or until the okra are soft.

~Serve with rice and fried fish.

Puerto Rico

Piononos

Deep-fried Plantain Rings with Ground Beef

SERVES 4

2 big, ripe plantains
1/4 cup butter or margarine
2 tsp vegetable oil
2 tbsp vegetable oil mixed with 1 tsp liquid annatto
1 lb lean ground beef
1 small onion, chopped
1/2 green pepper, chopped
1 fresh hot pepper, chopped
1 garlic clove, crushed
1 heaped tbsp plain flour
3 ripe tomatoes, skinned and chopped
3 tbsp water
1 tsp salt
freshly ground black pepper
1 1/2 tbsp vinegar
4 eggs
vegetable oil for frying

~Peel the plantains (see page 17).

~Heat the butter or margarine with the vegetable oil in a large frying pan. Cut each plantain lengthways into 4 thick slices. Cook them in the pan for 4 minutes, turning them over now and again until they have browned. Drain them on paper towels.

~Heat the annatto-flavored oil in the same pan over a medium heat, and add the beef, onion, green pepper, hot pepper, and garlic. Cook for 5 minutes.

~Add the flour and stir it in, then add the tomatoes, water, salt, and freshly ground black pepper to taste. Cook until the mixture thickens.

~Stir in the vinegar.

~To make piononos, carefully bend each plantain slice around into a ring about 3 inches in diameter, securing the overlapping ends with a wooden toothpick. Lay the rings side by side.

~Spoon the beef mixture into each ring, and press the tops as flat as possible.

~Beat the eggs and brush some over the piononos.

~Heat enough oil in a large pan to deep-fry the piononos. Fry them for about 3 minutes each side, turning them over very gently. Drain them on paper towels, and serve as soon as they are all cooked.

~Serve with rice 'n' peas or Black Beans and Rice (see page 86).

85

Left *Piononos served with rice and garden peas – an alternative to traditional rice 'n' peas.*

Vegetables and Pulses

Black Beans and Rice

SERVES 6

1¼ cups dried black beans
12 cups water
3 tbsp vegetable oil
1 small onion, chopped
1 garlic clove, chopped
½ green pepper, chopped
1¼ cups uncooked long-grain white rice
1 tsp salt
freshly ground black pepper

~ Rinse the beans in a colander under cold running water until the water runs clear.

~ Bring 10 cups of the water to the boil in a large saucepan, add the beans, reduce the heat, and then simmer for approximately 3 hours or until the beans are cooked.

~ Drain the beans in a colander. Mash 2 tablespoons of the beans to a smooth paste with a fork.

~ Heat the oil in a large frying pan. Add the onion, garlic and green pepper, and cook them until soft.

~ Stir in the bean paste, and then add the rest of the beans. Reduce the heat and simmer, uncovered, for 10 minutes.

~ Return the contents of the frying pan to the large saucepan. Add the rice, salt and remaining water, bring to the boil, then reduce the heat, cover, and simmer for 20 minutes or until the rice is cooked.

~ Season to taste with salt and freshly ground black pepper.

86

Above *Fishermen on Varadero Beach, Cuba.*

Martinique

Eggplants in Coconut Sauce

2 lb eggplants
1 tbsp salt
8 tbsp oil
2 onions, sliced
2 garlic cloves, crushed
6 tomatoes, skinned and chopped
1¼ cups coconut milk (see page 15)
freshly ground black pepper
2 tbsp shredded coconut

~Cut the eggplants into ½-inch thick slices. Place them in a colander, sprinkling a little salt over each layer of slices, and leave, weighted down with a plate, for 20 minutes. Rinse off the bitter juices that will have oozed out, and dry with paper towels.

~Heat 6 tablespoons oil in a large frying pan. Fry the eggplant slices for 10 minutes, turning them once during this time. Drain them on paper towels.

~Preheat the oven to 350°F.

~Heat the remaining oil in the same pan, add the onions, and fry for 5 minutes over a medium heat.

~Add the garlic and tomatoes, and cook for 3 minutes, stirring constantly.

~Pour in the coconut milk and season to taste with salt and freshly ground black pepper. Layer the eggplant slices in an ovenproof dish, then pour the coconut sauce over them. Cover with foil, and bake in the preheated oven for 30 minutes.

~Uncover, sprinkle with the shredded coconut, and bake for 5 more minutes.

Antigua

Sweet Potato and Walnut Soufflé

SERVES 6

4 small sweet potatoes
2 tbsp butter or margarine
2 tbsp flour
1 cup milk
½ small onion, grated
¼ tsp thyme
freshly ground black pepper
4 eggs, separated
1¼ cups walnuts, chopped

~Cook the sweet potatoes in boiling water until they are soft. Drain them and leave them to cool. Peel the sweet potatoes, then mash them with a fork.

~Preheat the oven to its lowest setting.

~In a saucepan, melt the butter or margarine, then stir in the flour. Gradually add the milk, stirring, and cook until the sauce thickens.

Remove the pan from the heat and add the onion, thyme, and freshly ground black pepper. Beat the egg whites until they are stiff, then gently fold them into the sauce.

~Add the walnuts and sweet potato, stirring them in gently. Beat the egg yolks and add these to the mixture. Pour the mixture into a greased soufflé dish. Bake in the preheated oven for 20 minutes, then serve immediately.

Left Eggplants in Coconut Sauce.

Barbados

Yam Soufflé

SERVES 4

3 small yams, peeled and quartered
¼ cup butter or margarine
1¼ cups milk
½ cup cheese, grated
1 tsp salt
2 eggs, separated
freshly ground black pepper

~Boil the yams until they are soft, then drain and mash them with a fork. Beat in the butter or margarine and gradually add the milk.

~Add half the cheese, the salt, egg yolks, and freshly ground black pepper to taste.

~Preheat the oven to 350°F, and grease a baking dish.

~Beat the egg whites until they are stiff and gently mix them into the yam mixture. Carefully spoon the mixture into the prepared baking dish. Sprinkle with the remaining grated cheese, and bake for 30 minutes until the top has gently browned. Serve at once.

Jamaica

Ackee and Salt Fish

SERVES 6

2 lb salt cod
¼ cup vegetable oil
1 onion, sliced
1 garlic clove, crushed
1 fresh hot pepper, chopped (see page 16)
2 tomatoes, skinned and chopped
14-oz can ackee

~Soak the cod overnight to remove the salt. Next day, drain it, then rinse it well under cold running water and break into flakes. Discard the skin and bones. Heat the oil in a frying pan, add the onion, garlic and hot pepper, and fry over a low heat until they are soft.

~Add the prepared salt cod and fry for 5 minutes, stirring constantly.

~Add the tomatoes, and cook for 5 more minutes.

~Add the ackee and cook until it looks like scrambled eggs, then serve.

~Serve hot with rice 'n' peas and fried plantains.

Right Ackee and Salt Fish served with rice and garden peas.

Barbados

Jug Jug

Pigeon Peas with Salt Beef and Cornmeal

SERVES 8

½ lb lean salt beef
3 cups dried pigeon peas
½ lb lean salt pork, cut into 5 pieces
7½ cups water
¼ cup yellow cornmeal
1 tsp thyme
⅓ cup butter or margarine
1 medium onion, chopped
salt and freshly ground black pepper

~Put the salt beef into a heavy saucepan with enough water to cover. Bring to the boil, then reduce the heat and simmer, covered, for about 3 hours.

~Drain the beef, then chop it coarsely.

~Wash the pigeon peas under cold running water, then put them, the salt pork, and water into a large saucepan. Bring to the boil, reduce the heat, then partially cover the pan and simmer for 2 hours.

~Drain, reserving the cooking liquid (you should have just over 3 cups, but if it is less, make it up to this amount with cold water). Chop the pork and peas coarsely. Return the cooking liquid to the pan and bring to the boil, then pour in the cornmeal and whisk it in. Add the thyme, and boil for 10 minutes until the mixture is thick.

~Melt a third of the butter or margarine in a large frying pan. Add the onion and cook for 5 minutes, stirring, until soft.

~Stir in the cornmeal-thickened sauce, pork and peas, and beef. Season to taste with salt and freshly ground black pepper, and simmer for 20 minutes. Stir in the remaining butter and serve at once.

Martinique

Baked Christophene

SERVES 4

2 christophenes
1 cup water
½ tsp salt
1 onion, chopped
1 tbsp butter or margarine
freshly ground black pepper
1 tsp breadcrumbs

~Preheat the oven to 350°F.

~Peel the christophenes, then cut them into small pieces and boil in the water, to which the salt has been added, until soft. Drain well, and mash with a fork.

~Add the onion, half the butter or margarine, and freshly ground black pepper.

~Grease a baking dish with the remaining butter or margarine, pour the mashed christophene into it, sprinkle with the breadcrumbs, and bake in the preheated oven for 15 minutes.

Above *Bridgetown, Barbados.*

Right *Baked Christophene.*

Desserts

Mango Mousse ~ Trinidad

Sweet Potato Flapjacks ~ Grenada

Banana Fritters ~ Martinique

Pumpkin Pie ~ Surinam

Guava Pie ~ Jamaica

Tropical Fruit Salad ~ St. Lucia

Soursop Ice Cream ~ Guyana

Coconut-Milk Sorbet ~ Barbados

Pineapple Fool ~ Jamaica

Baked Bananas Flambées ~ Antigua

Trinidad

Mango Mousse

SERVES 8

5 medium, ripe mangoes (see page 16)
3 tbsp lime or lemon juice
2 egg whites
pinch of salt
¼ cup sugar
6 tbsp heavy cream

~Dice the flesh of 2 of the mangoes, and purée the rest in a blender.

~Put the purée into a glass mixing bowl, and stir in the lime or lemon juice.

~Beat the egg whites with the salt until they are frothy. Sprinkle in the sugar, and continue to beat until stiff. Gently fold in the cream. Gradually stir the mixture into the mango purée. Pour over the diced mango. Spoon the mixture into serving bowls or glasses, and then chill for at least 3 hours before serving.

Grenada

Sweet Potato Flapjacks

SERVES 6

1 lb sweet potatoes
¾ cup butter or margarine
½ tsp salt
1 cup light brown sugar, firmly packed
2 eggs
½ tsp freshly grated nutmeg
½ tsp ground ginger
2 tbsp rum

~Preheat the oven to 350°F.

~Peel and grate the sweet potatoes.

~Cream the butter or margarine with the salt and gradually blend in the sugar. Beat until light and fluffy.

~Add the eggs, nutmeg, ginger, rum and grated sweet potato, mixing well. Spoon the mixture into a greased baking dish, smooth the top, and bake in the preheated oven for 60 minutes.

~Leave to cool, then cut it into slices.

~Serve with rum-flavored whipped cream.

Right Sweet Potato Flapjacks.

Martinique

Banana Fritters

SERVES 6

2 cups plain flour
pinch of salt
1 tsp baking powder
$^{1}/_{2}$ cup milk
1 egg
1 tbsp butter or margarine, melted
$^{1}/_{3}$ cup sugar
3 small, ripe bananas
3 tbsp light rum
2 tbsp lime or lemon juice
vegetable oil for frying
$^{1}/_{2}$ cup grated coconut or cheese

~ Make a batter by putting the flour, salt, baking powder, milk, egg, melted butter or margarine, and a third of the sugar in a blender and mixing it at high speed. Pour the batter into a bowl.

~ Peel the bananas and cut them into 1-inch slices. Mix them in a bowl with the rum, lime or lemon juice, and half the remaining sugar. Leave them to marinate for 1 hour.

~ Heat the oil in a little frying pan until it is very hot. Drain the banana slices, dip them into the batter, and fry until they are golden brown, then drain them on paper towels.

~ Sprinkle the grated coconut or grated cheese over the banana slices, and place under a hot grill for 2 minutes. Serve hot.

Surinam

Pumpkin Pie

SERVES 6

1 lb pumpkin
1 cup water
1 tbsp butter or margarine
2 eggs
$^{2}/_{3}$ cup milk
$^{1}/_{2}$ tsp freshly grated nutmeg
1 tsp cinnamon
$^{1}/_{3}$ cup sugar
9-in pastry piecrust, baked blind and cooled
(see page 100)

~ Peel the pumpkin and cut the flesh into cubes. Cook in the water until it is soft. Drain it, and mash it with a fork.

~ Preheat the oven to 450°F.

~ In a saucepan, melt the butter or margarine. Beat the eggs and mix in the milk, nutmeg, and cinnamon. Add this mixture to the melted butter or margarine, and cook over a medium heat for 15 minutes.

~ Pour in the sugar and mashed pumpkin, stir well together, and cook for 10 more minutes.

~ Remove the pan from the heat and leave to cool.

~ Spoon the pumpkin filling into the piecrust and bake in the preheated oven for 10 minutes, then lower the heat to 300°F and bake until firm.

Left Banana Fritters.

Guava Pie

MAKES ONE 23 cm/9 in PIE

2 × 2 lb 2 oz cans guavas
3 tbsp lime or lemon juice
2 tsp arrowroot, blended with 1½ tbsp cold water
9-in pastry piecrust, baked blind and cooled
1¼ cups chilled heavy cream, whipped
lime zest to decorate

~ Drain the guavas, reserving the liquid, and place them in a glass bowl on one side.

~ Pour the reserved guava liquid into an enamel saucepan and cook until it has reduced to ⅔ cup.

~ Add the lime or lemon juice and arrowroot mixture to the boiling liquid, stirring constantly until the mixture is thick.

~ Remove the pan from the heat and, using a pastry brush, coat the inside of the piecrust with a little over half of the mixture.

~ Place the guavas in the piecrust, then pour the remaining guava syrup over them and leave to cool at room temperature.

~ Serve with the whipped cream, and decorate with lime zest.

PIECRUST PASTRY

TO MAKE ONE 8–9-INCH PIECRUST

⅓ cup unsalted butter, chilled and cut into ¼-in pieces
2 tbsp lard, chilled and cut into
¼-in pieces
1½ cups plain flour
1 tbsp sugar
¼ tsp salt
2–3 tbsp iced water
1 tbsp butter (for a "blind" case)

~ Put the butter, lard, flour, sugar, and salt into a large, chilled bowl. Rub the flour and fats together with your fingertips until they look like fine breadcrumbs. Do not let the mixture become oily.

~ Pour 2½ tablespoons of iced water over the mixture, toss it together lightly, and gather it into a ball. If the dough crumbles, gradually add up to 2½ teaspoons more iced water. Dust the pastry dough with a little flour, and wrap it in waxed paper. Refrigerate for at least an hour before using.

~ To prepare a blind, or unfilled, baked piecrust, spread 1 tablespoon butter over the bottom and sides of a 9-inch pie dish. Pat the prepared dough into a rough circle about 1 inch thick on a floured surface. Dust a little flour over and under it, and roll it out from the center to within 1 inch of the far edge. Lift the dough and turn it clockwise about 2 inches; roll again from the center. Repeat until the dough is ⅛ inch thick and 13–14 inches in diameter.

~ Roll the dough onto a rolling pin and unroll it slackly over the pie dish. Cut off the excess dough, leaving 1 inch all around. Chill for 1 hour. Preheat the oven to 400°F. Spread a sheet of buttered aluminum foil across the dish, and press it gently into the edge of the piecrust. Bake on the middle shelf for about 10 minutes, then remove the foil. Prick the pastry, then return it to the oven for a further 10 minutes until it begins to brown. Remove and cool.

Tropical Fruit Salad

SERVES 6

1 fresh pineapple, peeled and sliced (see page 17), or
14-oz can pineapple slices
3 tbsp rum
¼ cup brown sugar
juice of 1 lemon
2 bananas, sliced
2 mangoes, sliced
2 ripe guavas, sliced
5 tbsp grated fresh coconut meat
½ tsp freshly grated nutmeg

~ Put the pineapple slices into a glass bowl. Add the rum and sugar and chill, covered, for 1 hour.

~ Pour in the lemon juice, and mix in all the fruit. Serve sprinkled with the grated coconut and nutmeg.

103

Above *Marie island cactus, St. Lucia.*

Guyana

Soursop Ice-cream

SERVES 4

1 medium soursop
2 cups water
2 × 14-oz cans condensed milk
1¼ cups evaporated milk
1 tsp butter or margarine
¼ tsp vanilla essence
sugar to taste
3 tbsp cornstarch

~Cut the soursop in half. Remove the flesh with a spoon and mix it with a quarter of the water. Press it through a sieve to extract the pulp.

~Mix the milks and remaining water in a saucepan and bring to the boil.

~Add the butter or margarine, vanilla essence, and sugar to taste.

~Mix the cornstarch with a little warm water, then add it to the mixture in the pan, stirring all the time until it thickens well. Remove the pan from the heat and leave to cool.

~Add the soursop pulp to the pan, mix it in well, then transfer to shallow freezer containers and freeze for 3 hours, beating it every 30 minutes or so to break down the ice crystals. Otherwise, follow the instructions if you have an ice cream maker. Remove the ice cream from the freezer at least 30 minutes before serving so it will be soft enough to serve.

Above *Kingstown market, St. Vincent.*

Barbados

Coconut-milk Sorbet

MAKES 2½ cups

1½ lb fresh coconut meat (see page 15)
2 cups milk, warmed
3 tbsp water
1 cup sugar
2 drops vanilla essence
fresh mint leaves to decorate

~ Preheat the oven to 350°F.

~ Grate a third (½ lb) of the coconut. Sprinkle it in a roasting pan, and roast in the preheated oven for 15 minutes or until it has lightly browned. Set it to one side.

~ Make coconut milk from the remaining coconut and the warm milk (see page 15).

~ Bring the water and sugar to the boil in a saucepan and heat until the sugar has dissolved, then leave it to cool.

~ Add the vanilla essence, coconut milk and roasted coconut to the syrup, stir well, then pour the mixture into 2 ice cube trays from which the dividers have been removed. Freeze the sorbet for 3 hours, stirring every 30 minutes to break up the large ice crystals. Sorbet should have a fine, firm texture when ready. Remove it from the freezer at least 30 minutes before serving so it will be soft enough to scoop out.

~ Serve in small bowls, decorated with the mint leaves.

Jamaica

Pineapple Fool

SERVES 4

¾ lb fresh pineapple, papaya or mango, finely chopped
(see pages 14–17)
1¼ cups heavy cream
½ tsp vanilla essence
3 tbsp powdered sugar

~ Drain the pineapple, papaya, or mango.

~ Whip the cream together with the vanilla essence and a third of the powdered sugar.

~ Chill the cream and pineapple, papaya, or mango separately for 1 hour.

~ Just before serving, fold the cream into the pineapple, papaya or mango, and serve at once in small bowls.

Baked Bananas Flambées

SERVES 4

4 large, ripe bananas
3 tbsp light rum
¼ cup butter or margarine
⅓ cup sugar
½ tsp ground allspice
2 tbsp fresh lime or lemon juice

~Preheat the oven to 400°F.

~Pierce the unpeeled bananas with a fork, place on a baking sheet, and bake in the preheated oven for 10–15 minutes or until soft.

~Leave them to cool, then peel off the skins.

~Warm the rum in a small frying pan.

~In another pan, melt the butter or margarine, then add the sugar and allspice and mix well. Coat the bananas in this mixture, and put each one in a serving dish. Sprinkle the lime or lemon juice over the bananas.

~Remove the pan with the rum from the heat, then set light to the rum with a match. Pour the flaming rum gently over the bananas, and serve immediately.

BANANAS
FROM THE
WINDWARD ISL

Breads and Cakes

CORNMEAL DUMPLINGS ~ Trinidad

SWEET CORN BREAD ~ Dominican Republic

COCONUT BREAD ~ Barbados

BANANA BREAD ~ Jamaica

CASSAVA BISCUITS ~ Barbados

COCONUT SUGAR CAKES ~ Antigua

BAKES ~ Trinidad

GÂTEAU DE PATATE ~ Haiti

CORN PONE ~ Barbados

CARIBBEAN CHRISTMAS PUDDING ~ All the Islands

Trinidad

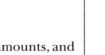

Cornmeal Dumplings

Dominican Republic

Sweet Corn Bread

MAKES 12 DUMPLINGS

¹/₃ cup yellow cornmeal
¹/₂ cup plain flour
1 tsp baking powder
1¹/₂ tsp salt
3 tbsp butter or margarine
3 tbsp cold water

~Sift the cornmeal, flour, baking powder, and a quarter of the salt into a large mixing bowl. Mix well, then rub in the butter or margarine until the mixture looks like breadcrumbs. Add just enough of the water to make a dough.

~Divide the dough into 12 equal amounts, and pat them into round dumplings.

~Bring 2 quarts of water, to which 1 teaspoon of salt has been added, to the boil. Drop the dumplings into the water, and stir once or twice to prevent them sticking to the bottom of the pan. Reduce the heat and simmer for 15 minutes, or until the dumplings swell and rise to the surface.

~Remove them to a warmed serving dish.

~Serve at once with chicken stew.

MAKES 2 LOAVES

²/₃ cup plus 1 tbsp butter or margarine
1¹/₄ cups plain flour
1³/₄ cups yellow cornmeal
2 tsp baking powder
¹/₂ tsp ground cinnamon
¹/₂ tsp freshly ground nutmeg
¹/₂ tsp ground cloves
¹/₃ cup coconut milk (see page 15)
¹/₃ cup milk
¹/₄ cup sugar
4 eggs
1¹/₄ cups fresh coconut meat, grated

~Preheat the oven to 400°F.

~Use 1 tablespoon of the butter or margarine to grease two 7 × 4 × 3-inch bread pans. Shake a little flour in each pan to coat.

~Sift the remaining flour, cornmeal, baking powder, cinnamon, nutmeg, and cloves together. Gradually mix in the coconut milk and milk.

~Cream the remaining butter or margarine with the sugar until it is light and fluffy. Beat in the eggs, one at a time. Gradually incorporate the cornmeal mixture and coconut.

~Pour the batter into the prepared pans, and bake in the center of the preheated oven for 35 minutes or until golden brown.

~Leave to cool in the pans for 5 minutes, then turn the loaves out onto wire racks to cool completely.

Above *Nutmegs drying.*

Right *Sweet Corn Bread.*

Barbados

Coconut Bread

Jamaica

Banana Bread

MAKES 3 SMALL LOAVES

¼ cup plus 1 tbsp butter or margarine
5 cups plain flour
1¾ cups sugar
2 tsp baking powder
½ tsp ground cinnamon
¼ tsp ground cloves
¾ tsp salt
1 large, fresh coconut, meat removed and finely grated
2 cups milk

~Preheat the oven to 350°F.

~Use 1 tablespoon of the butter or margarine to grease three 3½ × 7-inch bread pans. Shake a little flour in each pan to coat.

~Sift the remaining flour, sugar, baking powder, cinnamon, cloves, and salt into a deep mixing bowl. Add the grated coconut and mix everything together. Gradually incorporate the milk and remaining butter or margarine.

~Divide the batter between the prepared pans filling each one not more than two-thirds full, then bake in the center of the preheated oven for 1 hour or until the top is golden brown and crusty.

~Leave the loaves to cool in their pans for 5 minutes, then turn them out onto wire racks to cool completely.

MAKES 1 LARGE LOAF

½ cup plus 1 tbsp butter or margarine
½ cup unsalted, shelled peanuts or blanched almonds
¼ cup raisins
2 cups plain flour
2½ tsp baking powder
¼ tsp freshly ground nutmeg
½ tsp salt
2 large, ripe bananas
½ tsp vanilla essence
⅓ cup sugar
1 egg

~Preheat the oven to 350°F.

~Use 1 tablespoon of the butter or margarine to grease a 9 × 5 × 3-inch bread pan.

~Chop the nuts and mix them with the raisins.

~Sift the flour, baking powder, nutmeg, and salt together.

~Peel the bananas and coarsely chop them, then mash to a purée with a fork. Add the vanilla essence.

~Cream the remaining butter or margarine with the sugar in a large mixing bowl. Blend in the egg. Beat the flour and banana mixtures in alternately. Beat well until the batter is smooth.

~Add the nut and raisin mixture.

~Pour the batter into the prepared pan. Bake in the preheated oven for 1 hour.

~Leave the bread to cool in the pan for 5 minutes, then turn it out onto a wire rack to cool completely.

Right Banana Bread.

114

Barbados

Cassava Biscuits

MAKES 24

1 lb cassava
½ cup butter or margarine
⅓ cup sugar
1 egg
1 cup fresh coconut meat, grated and firmly packed
2 cups plain flour
1 tsp baking powder

~ Preheat the oven to 400°F.

~ Peel the cassava and grate the flesh. Squeeze off the juice (see page 15), and put the pulp to one side.

~ Cream the butter or margarine and sugar together.

~ Add the egg, grated cassava and coconut, and mix together well.

~ Mix the flour and baking powder together and sift them onto a sheet of waxed paper. Turn the creamed mixture out onto the paper and knead to incorporate the flour. When the dough is stiff, knead it for 2 or 3 more minutes, then roll it out to a thickness of about 1 inch. Using a floured 2-inch round cookie cutter, cut out the cookies and place them on a baking tray about 1 inch apart. Bake in the preheated oven for 20 minutes or until the cookies are golden brown.

Left Cassava Biscuits.

Antigua

Coconut Sugar Cakes

MAKES 15 CAKES

2 cups sugar
⅔ cup water
drop of red, yellow, or green food coloring (optional)
1¾ cups fresh coconut meat, grated
2 drops almond essence

~ Boil the sugar in the water until the sugar has dissolved. Add the food coloring, the coconut and almond essence, stirring all the time until the mixture becomes thick.

~ Remove the pan from the heat and beat the mixture for a few minutes.

~ Drop spoonfuls of the mixture onto a greased baking sheet. Leave to cool and harden.

117

Bakes

Fried Biscuits

MAKES 9 BISCUITS

2 cups plain flour
1½ tsp baking powder
1 tsp salt
2 tbsp butter, softened, or margarine
1½ tsp sugar dissolved in 3 tbsp cold water
vegetable oil for frying

~ Sift the flour, baking powder, and salt into a bowl. Add the butter or margarine, and rub together until the mixture looks like breadcrumbs.

~ Pour the sugar and water mixture into the bowl and mix to make a dough.

~ Form the dough into small balls, and flatten each into rounds about 3 inches in diameter.

~ Heat a little oil in a large frying pan, and fry the biscuits for about 3 minutes on each side. Transfer them to paper towels to drain.

Gateau de Patate

Sweet Potato Bread

SERVES 6

¹/₄ cup plus 1 tbsp butter or margarine
2 lb sweet potatoes, peeled and quartered
1 large, ripe banana, peeled and chopped
3 eggs, lightly beaten
1 cup sugar
scant ¹/₂ cup milk
³/₄ cup light corn syrup
generous ¹/₃ cup evaporated milk
¹/₄ tsp vanilla essence
¹/₄ tsp freshly ground nutmeg
¹/₄ tsp ground cinnamon
¹/₄ cup raisins

~Preheat the oven to 350°F.

~Use 1 tablespoon of the butter or margarine to grease a 9 × 5 × 3-inch bread pan.

~Boil the sweet potatoes in salted water until soft, then drain and mash them with a fork.

~Mash the banana pieces and mix with the sweet potato in a deep bowl.

~Add the remaining butter, eggs, sugar, milk, light corn syrup, evaporated milk, vanilla, nutmeg, cinnamon, and raisins to the bowl and beat well.

~Pour the batter into the prepared bread pan, and bake in the preheated oven for 1½ hours.

~Leave to cool for 5 minutes in the pan, and then turn the loaf onto a wire rack to cool completely.

~Serve with fresh cream.

Corn Pone

Cornmeal Cake with Raisins and Cherries

SERVES 8

1 cup butter or margarine
1¼ cups yellow cornmeal
2 cups plain flour
1 cup sugar
¼ tsp vanilla essence
¼ tsp freshly ground nutmeg
pinch of salt
6 eggs, lightly beaten
1¼ cups milk
1 tbsp light rum
¾ cup raisins

~Preheat the oven to 350°F.

~Use 1 tablespoon of the butter or margarine to grease a 8-inch round cake pan.

~Sift the cornmeal and flour together into a deep mixing bowl.

~Cream the remaining butter or margarine and sugar together. Add this to the cornmeal mixture, together with the remaining ingredients, and mix well until the batter is smooth.

~Pour the batter into the prepared pan, and bake in the preheated oven for 1½ hours or until the cake is golden brown. Leave it to cool for 5 minutes before turning it out of the pan and serving.

120

Carribbean Christmas Pudding

MAKES 2 PUDDINGS

1½ cups raisins
1½ cups currants
1⅓ cups stoned prunes, chopped
¾ cup mixed peel
1 cup candied cherries
1 tsp freshly grated nutmeg
1 tsp ground cinnamon
3¼ cups fresh, soft, white breadcrumbs
4 cups plain flour
1 tsp baking powder
1 cup sugar
1 cup butter or margarine
1¼ cups brandy
2 tsp vanilla essence
1 tsp almond essence
¼ cup orange juice
⅔ cup milk
½ cup ground almonds
3 tbsp ground cashew nuts
6 eggs, beaten

~In a large mixing bowl combine the raisins, currants, prunes, mixed peel, candied cherries, nutmeg, cinnamon, and breadcrumbs.

~Add the flour, baking powder, sugar and butter or margarine, and mix them together well.

~Add the brandy, essences, and orange juice. Mix again and leave to stand overnight.

~Next day, add the milk, nuts, and eggs.

~Pour the mixture into two 9 × 5 × 3-inch bowls that have been well greased and lined with waxed paper. Seal the bowls tightly with a dish towel tied around them to prevent water getting in. Place each pudding in a saucepan of boiling water, cover, and steam for 3 hours.

~When done, remove the bowls from the saucepans and leave to cool.

~Remove the puddings from the bowls and wrap in waxed paper, then in foil. Before serving, reheat in an oven or in a microwave oven, and serve with whipped cream.

Right *Caribbean Christmas Pudding.*

Indo-Caribbean Dishes

ROTI ~ Trinidad

GOAT CURRY ~ Jamaica

CHOKA ~ Guyana

SAHINA ~ Trinidad

POLOURI ~ Trinidad

CHICKEN PELAU ~ Trinidad

CRAB PELAU ~ Tobago

KACHOURI ~ Trinidad

BAIGANI ~ Trinidad

CURRIED LAMB WITH LENTILS ~ Surinam and Trinidad

Dhalpouri or Roti

Indian Bread stuffed with Split Pea Purée

> The Indian influence is more apparent in the cuisine of Jamaica, Trinidad, Guyana, and Surinam than it is in the cuisines of the other islands. Curry has become an integral part of Caribbean cooking. As a matter of fact, the national party dish of Jamaica is curried goat and rice. Rice and chicken curry or goat curry must be on the menu at every party! In Trinidad, pelau is the national dish. It is a beautiful saffron-colored rice dish with meat or seafood and is garnished with raisins and tomatoes.

124

SERVES 10

4 cups split peas
1 tbsp salt
1/2 tsp ground turmeric
1 tbsp cumin seeds
1/4 tsp chili powder (optional)
6 cups plain flour
6 tsp baking powder
1/4 cup ghee (clarified butter) or margarine
vegetable oil for frying

~Wash the split peas and put them in a saucepan full of water to which half of the salt and the turmeric have been added. Bring to the boil and cook for 10 minutes or until the split peas are half-cooked.

~Drain off the water and process the split peas in a blender or food processor to form a powder, not a paste.

~Add the cumin and chili, then set the mixture on one side.

~Sift the flour, the remaining salt, and the baking powder into a large mixing bowl.

~Mix in the ghee or margarine, working it in until it is well blended.

~Add just enough warm water, little by little, until you have a soft dough. Knead the dough for 5 minutes.

~Form the dough into small balls and set aside on a floured board. Flour your hands well and flatten the balls into thick rounds. Put 1 or 2 tablespoons of the split pea mixture into the center of each round and close the dough over it, making sure the mixture is sealed inside the dough. Then, roll each with a floured rolling pin on a floured board to make a circle about 5 inches in diameter and .75-inch thick.

~Brush the tops with oil and place them, oiled side down, on a hot griddle. Cook them for 3 minutes, brush their tops with oil and turn over. Cook both sides until they are lightly browned. Remove them to a clean dish towel and wrap to keep them warm.

~Serve with fish, meat, chicken, or vegetable curry.

Goat Curry

SERVES 6

3 lb goat meat, chopped
1 tbsp salt
3 garlic cloves, crushed
1 tbsp vinegar or 2 tbsp lime or lemon juice
1/4 cup vegetable oil
1 onion, sliced
1/2 tsp ground cumin
1/3 cup curry powder
1 large, fresh tomato, chopped
1 fresh hot pepper, sliced (see page 16)
pinch methi leaves, chopped, to garnish (optional)

~Put the goat meat into a glass bowl together with the salt, half the garlic, the vinegar or lime or lemon juice, and 2 tablespoons of cold water. Mix them together well and leave to marinate for 3 hours.

~Heat the oil in a large saucepan over a medium heat. Add the onion and remaining garlic, and fry for 2 minutes until golden brown.

~Add the cumin and curry powder, mixed in a little water, and cook for 2 more minutes.

~Add the meat and sauté for 5 minutes.

~Add the tomato and hot pepper, and bring to the boil. Lower the heat and simmer until the meat is tender.

~Garnish with chopped methi leaves.

~Serve with steamed rice.

Choka

Eggplant Chutney

SERVES 6

2 medium eggplants
2 garlic cloves
2 tbsp olive oil
1 onion, finely chopped
juice of 1/2 lemon or lime
1 fresh hot pepper, finely chopped
2 scallions, chopped
salt and freshly ground black pepper

~Wash the eggplants, and cut a 1-inch slit in each one. Slot a clove of garlic into each hole. Rub the eggplants with some olive oil and place them under a hot grill, cooking them until the skin is black and the flesh soft and mushy. Discard the garlic cloves. Remove the eggplants to a plate and leave to cool.

~Peel off the skins and mash the flesh with a fork.

~Add the remaining olive oil, onion, lemon or lime juice, hot pepper, scallions, and salt and freshly ground black pepper to taste. Mix thoroughly.

~Serve with rice and chicken or fish curry.

127

Left *Goat Curry.*

Sahina

Dasheen Leaf Fritters

MAKES 12

6 dasheen leaves or spinach leaves, washed
1 cup split pea meal
1 cup plain flour
1 tsp baking powder
1 tsp ground turmeric
pinch of salt
1 cup cold water
vegetable oil for frying

~Leave the leaves to dry for a few days until they have turned slightly brown.

~In a bowl, mix the split pea meal, flour, baking powder, turmeric, and salt. Mix well, then gradually add the water to form a smooth batter.

~Spread some batter over each leaf, and stack them on top of each other. When the stack is 3–4 inches thick (about 6 leaves), roll the leaves up along the longest edge like a jelly roll and slice the roll across.

~Heat a little oil in a large frying pan and fry the slices until they are crisp. Place them on some paper towels to drain.

~Serve with hot pepper sauce.

Above *Cattle and egrets, Trinidad.*

Polouri

Split Pea Fritters

MAKES 50

2 cups split pea meal
2 cups plain flour
1 tsp baking powder
1/2 tsp ground turmeric
1/2 tsp salt
1/2 cup cold water
vegetable oil for frying

~In a bowl mix the split pea meal, flour, baking powder, turmeric, and salt.

~Add the water gradually, mixing well, to form a smooth batter.

~Heat enough oil in a large frying pan to deep-fry the fritters.

~Drop spoonfuls of the batter into the oil, and fry for 5 minutes until they are golden brown. Remove the polouris and allow to drain on paper towels. Serve either hot or cold.

Right *Polouri.*

Trinidad

Chicken Pelau

Chicken with Rice and Pigeon Peas

SERVES 6

1 onion, chopped
2 garlic cloves
1 tbsp chopped fresh chives
1 tbsp chopped fresh thyme
2 celery sticks with leaves, chopped
4 tbsp water
fresh coconut meat from ¹/₂ coconut (see page 15),
chopped
liquid from fresh coconut (see page 15)
1-lb can pigeon peas, drained
1 fresh hot pepper
1 tsp salt
freshly ground black pepper
2 tbsp vegetable oil
2 tbsp sugar
3¹/₂ lb chicken, chopped
1 cup uncooked rice, washed and drained
1¹/₄ cups water

~ Grind the onion, garlic, chives, thyme, and celery with 4 tablespoons water in a blender or food processor. Empty the mixture into a large saucepan.

~ Make coconut milk using the coconut meat and liquid.

~ Add the coconut milk to the pan, together with the pigeon peas and hot pepper. Cook over a low heat for 15 minutes, then season with the salt and freshly ground black pepper to taste.

~ Heat the oil in a flameproof casserole. Add the sugar and heat until it begins to caramelize.

~ Add the raw chicken to the casserole, and cook for 15 minutes until it has browned. Stir in the pigeon pea mixture, rice and 1¹/₄ cups of water. Bring to the boil, reduce the heat, cover, and simmer for 20 minutes or until the rice and chicken are cooked. Discard the hot pepper before serving.

Tobago

Crab Pelau

Rice with Crab and Coconut Milk

SERVES 6

2 tbsp butter or margarine
2 tbsp vegetable oil
1 medium onion, chopped
1 garlic clove, chopped
¹/₂ tsp hot pepper, chopped (see page 16)
5 tsp curry powder
1³/₄ cups uncooked long-grain white rice, washed
3³/₄ cups coconut milk (see page 15)
1 tsp salt
freshly ground black pepper
1 lb fresh, canned, or frozen crabmeat
1 tbsp fresh lime
2 tbsp raisins

~ Melt the butter or margarine in a large saucepan over a medium heat. Add the oil, onion, garlic and hot pepper, and cook for 5 more minutes.

~ Add the curry powder and stir in, then add the rice and cook for 3 minutes.

~ Add the coconut milk, salt, and freshly ground black pepper to taste and bring to the boil over a high heat, then reduce the heat, cover, and simmer for 15 minutes.

~ Add the crabmeat and lime or lemon juice, and simmer for 5 more minutes or until the liquid has been absorbed. Decorate with the raisins and serve hot.

~ Serve with a cucumber salad.

131

Left *Chicken Pelau.*

Trinidad

Kachouri

Chickpea Fritters

MAKES 20

1 lb gram or chickpea dhal
4 scallions, chopped
1/2 hot pepper, chopped
1 tsp baking powder
pinch of salt
vegetable oil for frying

~ Soak the dhal in water overnight.

~ Next day, drain off the water and grind the dhal to a paste in a blender or food processor. Transfer the paste to a mixing bowl.

~ Add the scallions, hot pepper, baking powder and salt, and mix them well.

~ Shape the mixture into small balls. Heat enough oil in a large frying pan to deep-fry the fritters until they are golden brown. Place them on paper towels to drain.

Trinidad

Baigani

Eggplant Fritters

SERVES 6

2 lb eggplants or potatoes
1 tbsp salt
generous 3/4 cup plain flour
freshly ground black pepper
4 scallions, chopped
1/2 hot pepper, chopped
1/2 cup cold water
vegetable oil for frying

~ Cut the eggplants into 1/2-inch thick slices and layer in a colander, sprinkling a little of the salt over each layer, then leave, weighted down with a plate, for 20 minutes. Rinse off the bitter juices and pat dry with paper towels.

~ If using potatoes instead, simply slice thinly .

~ In a large mixing bowl, put the flour, black pepper, scallions, hot pepper and a pinch of salt, and mix well.

~ Gradually add the water to the bowl to make a smooth batter.

~ Heat enough oil in a large frying pan to deep-fry the eggplant or potato slices.

~ Dip the eggplant or potato slices in the batter and deep-fry until they are golden brown. Place on paper towels to drain, then serve hot.

~ Serve with tomato or coconut chutney.

Curried Lamb with Lentils

SERVES 6

2 tbsp oil
1 tbsp cumin seeds
1 tsp ground turmeric
1 large onion, chopped
2 garlic cloves, crushed
2-in length of root ginger, peeled and finely
chopped
2 lb boned lamb or goat meat, cubed
1 hot pepper, chopped
1 cup lentils, washed and drained
14-oz can tomatoes, drained and chopped
1 tsp salt
freshly ground black pepper
2½ cups cold water

133

~ Heat the oil in a flameproof casserole, then add the cumin, turmeric, onion, garlic, and ginger. Fry them for 5 minutes over a medium heat.

~ Add the lamb or goat meat and cook for 5 more minutes.

~ Stir in the hot pepper, lentils, tomatoes, salt, and freshly ground black pepper to taste. Add the cold water, bring to the boil, then lower the heat, cover, and simmer for 1 hour until the lamb or goat is tender and the sauce has become thick.

~ Serve with Roti (see page 124) or steamed rice and mango chutney.

Drinks

Peanut Punch

Pina Colada

Banana Daiquiri

Mawby

Rum Daisy

Passion Fruit Cocktail

Sorrel

Bossa Nova

Soursop Nectar

Ginger Beer

Peanut Punch

SERVES 4

⅓ cup smooth peanut butter or 1 cup roasted peanuts,
finely ground
14-oz can evaporated milk
14-oz can condensed milk
1 cup water
1 tbsp sugar (optional)
1 egg
rind of 1 lime or lemon
1 tsp vanilla essence
2 cups white rum or 1 cup milk (optional)

~Mix the peanut butter or ground peanuts with the evaporated milk.

~Add the condensed milk and water, and mix together well. Taste and, if it is not sweet enough, add the sugar.

~Beat the egg with the lime or lemon rind, then discard the rind.

~Add the egg mixture, vanilla, and rum or milk to the peanut and milk mixture.

~Bottle and chill.

~Serve with ice cubes.

136

Pina Colada

SERVES 2

2 tbsp coconut cream
3 tbsp rum
⅓ cup unsweetened pineapple juice
⅔ cup crushed ice
2 slices pineapple to decorate
2 cherries to decorate

~Blend all the ingredients, except the pineapple and cherries, together in a blender for 10 seconds.

~Serve in tall glasses with a straw, decorated with pineapple slices and cherries.

Banana Daiquiri

SERVES 4

juice of ½ lime or lemon
1 tsp sugar
½ cup banana, canned mango or pineapple, chopped
¼ cup white rum
12 ice cubes, crushed
4 cherries to decorate

~Blend all the ingredients, except the cherries, together with the ice.

~Serve in cocktail glasses decorated with cherries on cocktail sticks.

Right Pina Colada.

Mawby

SERVES 10

4 oz mawby bark
3 bay leaves
8 cups cold water
white sugar to sweeten

~ Put the mawby bark, bay leaves, and cold water into a large saucepan. Bring to the boil, then lower the heat and simmer for 10 minutes.

~ Leave to stand until it has cooled completely.

~ Strain out the bark and bay leaves, and refrigerate the liquid in bottles for use as required.

~ To prepare the drink, make a syrup by combining sugar and cold water, heat until the sugar dissolves, and cool again. Add some of the refrigerated soursop mixture, and serve with ice cubes. If you want the drink less bitter, just add less of the mawby mixture to the syrup.

Rum Daisy

SERVES 2

2 tbsp white rum
juice of 1/2 lemon
1 tbsp grenadine syrup
2 cherries to decorate
2 slices banana to decorate

~ Mix the liquid ingredients together and decorate the glasses with cherries and banana slices.

Passion Fruit Cocktail

SERVES 6

1/4 cup sherry
5 cups passion fruit juice
2 tsp angostura bitters
1 cup grapefruit juice
1 cup guava juice
1 cup lemon juice
1 cup rum
1/2 cup, lightly packed brown sugar

1 nutmeg, freshly grated
1 orange, thinly sliced
6 cherries to decorate

~ Blend together all the ingredients, except for the nutmeg, orange slices, and cherries. Serve in tall glasses decorated with a slice of orange, a cherry, and a sprinkling of grated nutmeg.

Sorrel

SERVES 10

1 lb fresh sorrel leaves or ¼ lb dry
2 bay leaves
3 whole cloves
1 small cinnamon stick
4 cups white sugar

~ Put the sorrel and bay leaves, cloves, cinnamon, and sugar into a large saucepan. Pour hot water over to cover the leaves and boil for 1 minute only.

~ Remove the pan from the heat and leave to cool. Let the pan stand overnight.

~ Next day, sieve out the leaves and spices and sweeten to taste, if necessary. Bottle and put 1 whole clove in each bottle. Cap the bottles and leave to stand for 4 days. Chill and serve with ice cubes.

139

Opposite *Passion Fruit Cocktail.*
Left *Sorrel.*

Bossa Nova

SERVES 2

2 tbsp dark rum
1 1/2 tsp lime juice
1 1/2 tsp lemon juice
1 tbsp passion fruit juice
2 slices orange to decorate
2 slices lime to decorate

~Shake all the ingredients, except the orange and lime slices, together well and serve in tumblers with crushed ice. Decorate with slices of orange and lime.

Soursop Nectar

140

SERVES 4

1 large soursop
1 cup cold water
1 cup milk or light cream
3/4 cup plus 2 tbsp sugar

~Peel the soursop and put the pulp, together with the seeds, into a big sieve over a bowl. Press it with a spoon until all the liquid has been pressed out of the pulp and into the bowl.

~Pour the water, milk or cream, sugar, and soursop liquid into a blender and blend for 10 seconds.

~If the nectar is too sweet, add some more milk or cream and a drop of lime or lemon juice.

~Serve chilled.

Ginger Beer

SERVES 6

4-oz piece fresh root ginger
juice of 1 lime or lemon
3 whole cloves
4 cups sugar
10 cups water

~ Peel the root ginger and slice it thinly.

~ Put the ginger slices, together with the lime or lemon juice, cloves, and sugar in the cold water in a saucepan, bring to the boil, and boil for 5 minutes.

~ Remove the pan from the heat and leave to stand overnight.

~ The next day, sieve and taste it. If it is not sweet enough, add more sugar; if it is too sweet, add more water. Bottle the ginger beer, adding a whole clove to each bottle. Cap the bottles and leave them to stand for 5 days. Chill and serve with ice cubes.

141

Left *Bossa Nova.*

Index

142

143

Picture Credits

Quarto would like to thank the following for providing photographs and for permission to reproduce copyright material. While every effort has been made to acknowledge all copyright holders, we would like to apologize should any omissions have been made.

p4: John Dakers/Life File; *p9:* Grenada Board of Tourism; *p11:* Juliet Highet/Life File; *p12:* Allan Gordon/Life File; *p13:* Jeremy Hoare/Life File; *p14:* Andy Kidd/Life File; *p18:* Paul Richards/Life File; *p30:* Juliet Highet/Life File; *p34:* Andy Teare/Life File; *p38:* Peter Phipp/Travel Pictures; *p42:* Juliet Highet/Life File; *p54:* Paul Richards/Life File; *p64:* George Leaney/Life File; *p66:* Grahame A Singleton/Life File; *p72:* Lionel Moss/Life File; *p80:* Grenada Board of Tourism; *p86:* Jeremy Hoare/Life File; *p92:* Peter Phipp/Travel Pictures; *p94:* Jeremy Hoare/Life File; *p103:* Paul Richards/Life File; *p104:* Peter Phipp/Travel Pictures; *p110:* Peter Phipp/Travel Pictures; *p112:* Grenada Board of Tourism; *p122:* Peter Phipp/Travel Pictures; *p128:* George Leaney/Life File; *p134:* Paul Richards/Life File.